The Adaptive Professional

How to Stay Relevant and Human in the Age of AI

David G. Gatchell

Best-selling author of
Steps to Prosperity

Four Gifts Publishing
Austin, Texas

The Adaptive Professional: How to Stay Relevant and Human in the Age of AI

Four Gifts Publishing, Austin, TX

This book was created with the assistance of AI tools for writing, research, and cover graphics, with all ideas, decisions, and final editing completed by the author.

ISBN Number 979-8-9867200-4-3 (paperback)
ISBN Number 979-8-9867200-5-0 (e-book)
Library of Congress Classification Number HF5548.32 .G38 2025

Printed in the United States of America

Dedication

To everyone who has ever felt left behind by change, this book is for you.

"It is not the strongest of the species that survive, nor the most intelligent, but the one most responsive to change."
– Charles Darwin

"The measure of intelligence is the ability to change."
– Albert Einstein

"The future belongs to those who learn more skills and combine them in creative ways."
– Robert Greene

"All change is hard at first, messy in the middle, and gorgeous at the end."
– Robin Sharma

"We cannot become what we need to be by remaining what we are."
– Max De Pree

May you find the courage to take your first step,
the curiosity to keep learning,
and the confidence to know you still have something uniquely human to offer.

TABLE OF CONTENTS

Introduction

When I first started writing this book, I thought a lot about fear. Fear of change. Fear of being replaced. Fear of being left behind.

These fears aren't irrational, they're human. And right now, artificial intelligence seems to trigger all of them at once. Every headline screams about jobs disappearing, skills becoming irrelevant, or a future controlled by machines. No wonder so many people feel uneasy.

But here's the truth: change has always come for us. We've lived through the printing press, the steam engine, electricity, computers, and the internet. Each era stirred panic, but each also opened doors to new opportunities we couldn't imagine at the start. The people who thrived weren't always the smartest or the most experienced, they were the ones who chose to adapt.

This book isn't a technical manual or a hype piece for the latest tool. It's a story, a parable, about a mid-career professional named Alex who feels exactly what so many of us feel: the ground shifting under his feet. Through his journey, you'll see the struggles, the mistakes, the skepticism, and, most importantly, the small wins that transform fear into confidence.

You'll also see practical steps woven into his story: how to try AI for yourself, how to use it responsibly, and how to build fluency without losing what makes you uniquely human. Alex takes notes along the way, just like you might. By the end, you'll have both his story and his lessons in hand.

The appendices at the end of this book are designed to reinforce your learning and give you practical tools you can use right away. They serve as a bridge from the story to real-world action, helping you continue your growth long after you've turned the final page. These include:

- Appendix A: Lessons Learned
- Appendix B: Quick Start Guide to ChatGPT
- Appendix C: Productive Prompts for Reinvention
- Appendix D: Adaptive Action Plan

Throughout the story, you'll see references to both specific AI tools like ChatGPT and more general categories of tools. That's intentional. While ChatGPT appears often as an example, many similar AI assistants or chatbots exist, and new ones are emerging all the time. When the story uses broader terms like "AI tool," it's a reminder that you're not limited to any one app. Use these moments to explore the "AI Tools Quick Reference" in the appendix or to look up newer tools that may better fit your needs. The tools will change, but the adaptable mindset you build is what truly lasts.

My hope is simple: that this book eases some of your fear, sparks your curiosity, and reminds you that you're not too late, too old, or too far behind to thrive in the age of AI.

Because the future doesn't belong to the machines.

It belongs to the adaptive professional.

— *David Gatchell*

Chapter 1: Rumblings of Change

Alex Harper sat frozen at his desk, rereading the headline on his computer screen for the third time. "ChatGPT AI Passes CPA Exam with Flying Colors," it declared. His heart skipped a beat. As a certified public accountant with over a decade of experience, Alex had spent countless hours studying for those brutal exams. Now an artificial intelligence had aced them with an 85% average score, far surpassing the threshold for passing. If a machine could do that, what did it mean for him?

He scrolled through the article with a mix of awe and dread. The piece explained how the newest version of ChatGPT, a cutting-edge AI, had outsmarted its prior version and passed not only the CPA exam but also other accounting certifications. Alex felt a slight chill. The researchers quoted in the article didn't mince words: they suggested that programmers would soon create applications allowing computers to perform tasks currently done by humans, warning that ChatGPT "likely will prove disruptive to the accounting and auditing industries". Those words lingered, heavy with implication. Disruptive to the accounting industry. His industry.

He pushed his chair back and exhaled slowly, running a hand through his short brown hair. In the background, the office hummed with its usual Monday morning activity, phones ringing, printers churning, colleagues tapping away at spreadsheets. Normally, these familiar sounds comforted him. Today, they barely registered.

Just last week, Alex's close friend Mark had been laid off from his job at a local bank. Mark wasn't an accountant, but he'd been a back-office operations guy, handling tasks that were increasingly automated. The layoff hit Mark hard, and Alex had spent the weekend listening to him worry about what came next. Mark kept saying, *"They don't need people like me anymore; a computer can do what I do."* At the time, Alex tried to reassure his friend, but now he wasn't so sure. If AI could pass the CPA exam, how long before companies decided they didn't need people like *him* anymore?

A new email notification pinged on Alex's screen, momentarily pulling his attention. It was from Mr. Morales, the CEO of McAllister & Lee CPAs, the mid-sized accounting firm where Alex worked. Ten years ago the founder-led firm was struggling and Javier Morles was brough in as CEO to drive growth. Since then he has averaged 20% growth per year and founders and shareholders are all highly satisfied with his performance.

The subject line read: "Staff Meeting, Future Skills Initiative." Curious, Alex opened it and quickly scanned the contents. The firm had scheduled an all-hands meeting for Friday to discuss "emerging technologies in accounting, including AI tools, and the skills staff will need to adapt."

Alex swallowed hard. *It's happening.* The leadership at his firm clearly felt the tremors of change too. They were talking about adaptation, about skills, code words that made him think of *restructuring* and *efficiency*. The meeting sounded proactive and upbeat on the surface, but he read between the lines: *we all need to up our game, or else.*

His stomach did a little flip of anxiety. He had always considered himself a competent accountant, thorough with numbers, good with clients, decent with Excel. But he wasn't particularly "techie." Sure, he used the standard accounting software and could navigate a spreadsheet like a pro, but the world of artificial intelligence was foreign territory. The most advanced tech he'd used recently was an upgraded cloud-based bookkeeping system that automated some data entry. AI that could actually *think* and solve problems? That was something he'd only seen in sci-fi movies.

Across the open-plan office, Alex noticed his colleague Jason emerging from the break room with a mug of coffee. Jason was in his late twenties, one of the younger hires at the firm. He had a reputation for being tech-savvy, always talking about the latest app or gadget. If anyone in the office was already playing around with AI tools, it would be Jason. Alex considered waving him over to chat about the email, but hesitated. *What would I even ask? "Hey, are robots coming for our jobs?"* He didn't want to sound paranoid.

Instead, Alex stood up and decided to get some coffee himself. Maybe a brief chat would naturally turn to the topic. He grabbed his mug and walked to the break room, trying to compose his thoughts. The aroma of freshly brewed coffee usually perked him up; today it barely registered.

Jason was stirring sugar into his cup when Alex entered. "Morning, Jason," Alex said, forcing a casual tone.

"Morning! You see this?" Jason tapped his phone, which displayed the same headline Alex had just been agonizing over.

"Yeah," Alex replied, his voice neutral. "Hard to miss."

Jason grinned in that excited way of his. "Pretty wild, huh? An AI passed the CPA exam. I read that it not only passed, but it also did really well. They said it averaged like 85% or something insane."

Alex managed a thin smile. "I saw. It's impressive… and a little unnerving."

Jason took a sip of coffee. "I get it. But honestly, I think it's cool. Means less grunt work for us down the line. Imagine not having to comb through endless receipts or manually reconcile every entry. We could focus on the interesting stuff."

"Maybe," Alex allowed. The thought of offloading tedious tasks was appealing, he had to admit. He'd pulled his share of late nights crunching numbers in spreadsheets. Still, he couldn't shake the image of accountants being replaced wholesale. "But what if it goes beyond grunt work? That article talked about it being disruptive. What if our clients start using AI instead of calling us for advice?"

Jason shrugged. "Tools like ChatGPT can answer questions, sure. But they don't have the personal touch. I mean, would you trust a chatbot to give you nuanced business advice? I wouldn't, not without a human double-checking." He leaned against the counter, warming to the subject. "From what I've read, AI is great at handling *tasks*, not entire *jobs*. It can streamline stuff, but someone still needs to interpret the results, right? At least for now."

Alex nodded slowly. "Right… for now." It was a fair point. Even if AI could produce analysis or draft a report, a client might still want a human accountant to explain what it all meant for their business, to discuss strategy, to answer follow-up questions. Those human elements, judgment, trust, communication, were harder for a machine to replicate.

Still, *for now* echoed ominously in Alex's mind. He glanced at Jason's phone again. "What else did it say, the article?"

Jason unlocked his screen and scrolled. "They quoted some professor saying it'll change what we do, but it's not going to outright replace us. At least not in the short term. Something like, jobs will adapt rather than vanish." He found the line and paraphrased, "'People predicted the end of accountants with every new tech, computers, spreadsheets, you name it, but it didn't happen. Professions change and adapt.'"

That sounded a bit reassuring. Alex felt a small knot in his chest loosen. "I hope they're right," he said quietly.

Jason flashed an encouraging smile. "Hey, adaptation's the name of the game. Look at it this way, Alex: this could be an opportunity. If we learn to use these AI tools, we could get more done in less time. Maybe even go home earlier for once." He chuckled.

The thought of fewer late nights at the office was certainly appealing. Alex tried to imagine an AI handling the tedious parts of an audit or generating a first draft of a financial statement, leaving him to just review and polish. It would be nice to focus on higher-level analysis instead of ticking boxes and cross-checking numbers for hours. "Better work-life balance… that would be something," he mused.

Jason raised his mug in a mock toast. "To new technology making our lives easier."

Alex clinked his mug to Jason's, but he couldn't muster the same enthusiasm. "To hoping," he replied.

Back at his desk, Alex noticed a few other coworkers murmuring and gesturing at their screens. Clearly, he wasn't the only one who'd seen the news or the meeting announcement. A buzz was building in the office. Normally,

Monday morning chatter here revolved around weekend stories or dreaded deadlines. Today, it was all about AI, whispers of *"did you see that AI thing?"* and *"what's this meeting about?"* drifting across the cubicles.

He sank into his chair and took a gulp of coffee, now lukewarm. The prospect of Friday's meeting unsettled him. Would it be a pep talk about embracing new tools? A warning that the firm needed to modernize to survive? Perhaps Mr. Morales would even demonstrate some new AI software they were investing in. Alex's mind spun elaborate scenarios, none of them particularly calming.

A small part of him considered an escape route: *I could start looking for a new job, maybe something in a smaller firm or a different field entirely.* But he quickly dismissed the thought. Jumping ship because of a looming technology wave didn't guarantee safety; AI was a tide that would touch every shore sooner or later. And he actually liked his job here most days. McAllister & Lee was a respectable firm with good people. He had built relationships with colleagues and clients. The idea of leaving all that because he was afraid of a new tool felt premature, and cowardly.

No, he would have to face this head-on. He would attend that meeting Friday and find out what management had to say. In the meantime, perhaps he should start educating himself, if only to quell his anxiety. But where to begin? Alex wasn't even sure he fully understood what "AI" encompassed. Was ChatGPT the same as the AI used in self-driving cars or those algorithms that recommended movies? It all blurred together in his head as "advanced computer stuff."

He sighed and pulled out his spiral-bound notebook from a desk drawer, a habit he never dropped, even in this digital age.

Flipping to a fresh page, he jotted down a quick note to himself.

> Research how AI is impacting accounting jobs

It felt better putting a task in writing. This was how he tackled any unfamiliar problem in work: break it down, research, make a plan. Treat this looming AI disruption the same way, he told himself. He may not be tech-savvy yet, but he was a good researcher and a quick study when he set his mind to it.

As he capped his pen, Alex surveyed the note. It was a simple first step, but it grounded him. He would gather facts before Friday's meeting. Perhaps data and knowledge would replace some of the fear of the unknown with clarity. And if the news was grim, well, at least he wouldn't be blindsided.

Tucking the notebook aside, Alex returned to the spreadsheet open on his computer. It was a client's quarterly financial report he'd been working on. For now, the formulas and figures on the screen were comfortingly familiar. He began typing in numbers and adjusting entries, trying to re-focus on the immediate task. Yet, at the back of his mind, the reality was clear: change was coming, whether he liked it or not. He felt compelled to jot down a couple more notes.

> AI passed the CPA exam... Could it take my job next?
>
> Adapt or get left behind. Time to learn about this technology.

Chapter 2: First Encounters with AI

That evening, after the house had gone quiet, Alex opened his laptop at the kitchen table. A half-finished cup of chamomile tea sat beside it, wisps of steam curling upward. His daughter was in her room and his wife, Maria, glanced over from the couch where she was reading. "Working late again?" she asked softly.

"Not exactly," Alex said, offering a small smile. "Just...checking something out." He hesitated, then admitted, "I'm going to try that ChatGPT thing. You know, the AI everyone's talking about."

Maria bookmarked her page and set her book down. "Oh, the one from the news? Good idea. Let me know how it goes," she said encouragingly. Maria wasn't as rattled by the AI headlines as Alex was, she worked as a graphic designer freelance, and while AI tools were emerging in her field too, she hadn't yet felt personally threatened. Still, she understood Alex's worries and supported him exploring this new tech.

Alex navigated to the ChatGPT website. He realized he needed an account to use it. *Okay, first step, sign up.* He clicked "Sign Up" and entered his email, created a password, and verified his account. The process was straightforward, much like signing up for any online service. Soon, he was greeted with a simple web interface: a chat box waiting for his input, and a brief message explaining how he could type a question.

A small popup offered a tour of the interface and mentioned an upgrade to ChatGPT Plus for faster responses and access to more advanced capabilities. Alex skimmed it but decided to stick with the free version for now. He wasn't ready to invest money before even knowing what the AI could do for him.

His fingers hovered over the keyboard. *What should I ask it?* He felt almost self-conscious, as if he were about to talk to a stranger. The blinking cursor in the empty chat box was both inviting and intimidating.

He started with something simple and work-related that wouldn't reveal any sensitive information, no way was he going to test it with real client data right off the bat. After a moment's thought, Alex typed: "What is accrual accounting? Explain it in simple terms."

It was a basic question, something he knew like the back of his hand, but he wanted to see how the AI explained a fundamental concept. He hit Enter.

Almost instantly, a new message began to appear in the chat window, as if an invisible student were rapidly typing on the other end:

ChatGPT: "*Accrual accounting is an accounting method where revenues and expenses are recorded when they are earned or incurred, not when cash actually changes hands. In simple terms, it means you recognize money you're supposed to receive or pay out even before the money moves. For example, if you did a job in June but won't get paid until July, accrual accounting would still count that as revenue for June. This method gives a more accurate picture of a company's financial health during a given period, because it shows all the money earned and owed in that period, regardless of when cash comes in or goes out.*"

Alex blinked at the screen. The explanation was clear and concise, exactly how he might have explained accrual accounting to a client who didn't have an accounting background. It even used a friendly example about doing a job in June but getting paid in July. He was impressed. No jargon, no unnecessary detail, just a straightforward answer in plain English.

"Wow," he murmured.

"What did it say?" Maria called from the couch, sensing his intrigue.

He read the response out loud to her. "That's a pretty good explanation," she remarked. "I understood it perfectly, and you know I usually glaze over when you talk accounting." She gave him a playful wink.

Encouraged, Alex thought of another test. He recalled a task from earlier in the week, he had to explain to a small business client why their cash flow didn't match their profit. It was essentially an accrual vs. cash accounting discussion. He had managed it, but it took a few emails and a phone call to get the idea across. *What if I had used this explanation?* he thought. It would have saved time.

He typed a follow-up into ChatGPT: "Why can a company have profit but no cash? Explain in simple terms."

Again, ChatGPT's reply came swiftly:

ChatGPT: *"It's possible for a company to show a profit on paper but have little cash in the bank. This often happens due to the difference between profit (which is calculated under accrual accounting) and cash flow. For instance, imagine you made a lot of sales and sent out invoices. Those sales count as revenue, which helps increase profit, but if your customers haven't paid yet, you don't have the cash. Similarly, you might have expenses recorded (like bills you owe) that reduce profit, even if you haven't actually paid them yet. Other things can cause profit and cash to differ too, like buying a lot of inventory (you spend cash now, but haven't recorded it all as expense yet) or paying off old bills. In short, profit is an accounting concept that includes money* owed *to you and expenses you* owe *to others, while cash is what's actually in your account right now."*

Alex found himself nodding as he read the answer. It was accurate and digestible. This took him maybe ten seconds to get, whereas writing up such an explanation from scratch could have easily taken him fifteen minutes of careful wording. He couldn't exactly send a client an AI-generated explanation without review, of course, he'd need to double-check it and tailor it to the client's specifics, but as a starting point? This was promising.

Maria had gotten up and come to stand behind Alex, peering at the screen. "It's like you have a little teacher or assistant in there," she said. "No wonder people are excited about this."

"Yeah," Alex said quietly. "It's like an assistant." He liked that word, assistant. Not replacement. An assistant to handle the initial legwork of explanations.

Feeling a bit bolder, Alex decided to try something more directly useful to his own daily work. He opened a document containing a dense paragraph from a new lease accounting standard update he needed to summarize for a client. The text was full of legalistic language and technical terms that even he had to read twice to fully grasp. Copying the paragraph, he pasted it into the chat box (careful that it contained no client names or confidential numbers, just generic regulatory text) and typed: "Summarize the following text in plain language:" then hit Shift+Enter to add a newline, pasted the paragraph, and pressed Enter.

The AI processed for a couple of seconds longer this time, presumably digesting the longer input. Then it began to output a summary:

ChatGPT: *"In plain language, the new lease accounting standard says that if your business is renting something (like equipment or a building), you need to record that rent agreement on your balance sheet. In other words, you'll list what you have to pay in the future as a liability (a kind of IOU) and the right to use that asset (the thing you're renting) as an asset on your books. The goal is to make sure that companies show these rent obligations openly in their financial statements. This means no more keeping big lease debts hidden off the books. Everything has to be included so investors can see the full picture of what the company owes."*

As he read through the summary, a grin slowly spread across Alex's face. That clunky, complex paragraph had just been distilled into a clear explanation. It even pulled out the essential point, put leases on the balance sheet so obligations aren't hidden. He would, of course, double-check the accuracy against the original text, but on a quick read it looked spot on. This could save him so much time when preparing client memos or internal summaries.

Maria gently squeezed his shoulder. "I haven't seen you smile at your laptop during work in a while."

Alex exhaled a laugh. "I'm just thinking how much time something like this could give back. Remember last month when I spent hours drafting that email to explain the lease rule change to my client? This basically did the heavy lifting in seconds."

"That *is* amazing," Maria said. She returned to the couch, leaving Alex to explore further.

Alex's mind raced with possibilities. If it could summarize text and explain concepts, what about writing? He decided to attempt something he often found tedious: composing formal emails. One of the more time-consuming parts of his job was drafting polite, clear emails to clients or colleagues for various situations, reminding someone of an overdue invoice, requesting missing documents, or delivering a summary of findings. He often labored over the wording to get the tone just right.

He typed a new prompt: "Draft a polite email to a client named John explaining that his payment is 30 days overdue, and asking if he needs any help or has questions about the invoice." Again, ChatGPT whirred into action:

"Subject: Reminder: Invoice 1023, Payment Overdue

Dear John,

I hope you are well. I am writing to remind you that invoice 1023, dated May 1, is now 30 days past due. The total amount of $5,000 was due on June 1.

If you have already sent payment, please disregard this reminder. Otherwise, please let us know if there are any issues or questions regarding the invoice. We understand that sometimes paperwork slips through the cracks, or there may be concerns we can help address.

Please feel free to reach out if you need a copy of the invoice or if you have any questions. We value our relationship with you and want to ensure everything is in order.

Thank you for your prompt attention to this matter.

Sincerely,

Alex Harper
Senior Accountant
McAllister & Lee CPAs"

Alex read the draft, thoroughly impressed. It was polite, professional, and hit all the right notes, reminded the client of the overdue payment without sounding accusatory, offered help, and kept a friendly tone. He would tweak a few minor details (for instance, he might soften "30 days past due" to "a little past due" depending on the client relationship, and ensure the contact details matched the firm's format), but the bulk of the work was done. And it took him mere seconds to generate.

He copied the email text and pasted it into a blank document to save for later reference. If nothing else, it was a great starting template.

Of course, a cautious voice in the back of his mind reminded him: *Don't get carried away.* He knew he'd have to carefully review anything the AI produced. It was powerful, yes, but not infallible. He'd heard mentions that these models could sometimes produce errors or "hallucinate" false information. Though in these simple tests everything looked correct, he was dealing with fairly straightforward facts and general knowledge. In more complex scenarios, say, calculating a tricky tax adjustment or interpreting an unusual regulation, he'd need to double-check every output.

Still, the potential was undeniable. In a matter of minutes, ChatGPT had accomplished tasks that would have collectively taken him an hour or more to do from scratch.

Alex sat back and rubbed his eyes, feeling a mix of relief and cautious excitement. The initial fear he'd felt in the office earlier was tempered now by a budding sense of opportunity. Maybe Jason was right, maybe this tool could make his work-life easier, not destroy it. If he could delegate the first draft of an email, the initial pass at explaining a concept, or the summarizing of a technical memo to an AI, that could free up a lot of time. Time he could spend on deeper analysis, or on face-to-face meetings with clients, or heck, get home in time to have dinner with the family more often.

He closed the laptop for now, brain buzzing with ideas. Tomorrow at work, perhaps he'd try using ChatGPT for a real task, discreetly, of course. He wasn't sure how management would feel about staff using an AI tool for client work. The upcoming Friday meeting might clarify that. But as long as he kept client data confidential and just used it as a general assistant, it couldn't hurt to experiment a little.

Before heading to bed, Alex flipped open his trusty notebook and made a couple of quick journal-style entries to capture his thoughts:

> First try with ChatGPT, surprisingly good at plain English explanations.
>
> Drafted an email in seconds. Huge time saver, but must verify details.

He underlined "must verify" twice. That was an important point, he couldn't let the allure of speed make him sloppy. But with careful use, this AI assistant might just become his secret weapon at work.

Feeling more optimistic than he had in days, Alex went to join Maria, who was waiting by the stairs. As they headed up to bed, he found himself actually looking forward to tomorrow. It wasn't that all his worries had vanished, but now he had a plan: he would test AI's capabilities further and see where it could genuinely help. He would adapt, one step at a time.

Chapter 3: Trial and Error

Sunlight spilled through the slats of the office blinds as Tuesday morning got underway. Alex arrived at work a bit early, energized by last night's discoveries. He settled into his cubicle with a fresh determination. Today, he would put ChatGPT to use on actual work tasks, carefully, of course.

First, he glanced around to ensure a bit of privacy. A few early birds were in, but the office wasn't fully buzzing yet. He opened his browser and navigated to the ChatGPT site, logging in to the account he'd created. For a moment, he considered whether the firm might frown upon using an external AI tool. *Better keep it discreet until I know more.* He resized the window so it didn't fully cover his screen, making it easier to hide if needed.

His first test was something small. One of his to-do items this morning was drafting a short blurb for the firm's monthly client newsletter. Each month, the partners liked to include a "financial tip of the month" or a brief article on a relevant topic. Alex had been asked to write a paragraph or two about the importance of keeping personal and business finances separate for small business owners, a common issue they saw with some clients.

Normally, Alex would spend a good 30 minutes crafting a clear, friendly tip with examples. Today, he decided to have ChatGPT assist. He typed into the chat box: "Write a one-paragraph friendly tip for small business owners on why they should keep personal and business finances separate."

He hit Enter and watched. Within seconds, the AI produced a well-written paragraph:

ChatGPT: "*Tip of the Month: Always keep your personal and business finances separate. Mixing the two can lead to confusion, inaccurate records, and headaches during tax time. By opening a dedicated business bank account and using it for all business income and expenses, you'll have clear records and a better picture of how your business is doing. This separation not only makes bookkeeping easier, but it also protects you legally by reinforcing the boundary between you as an individual and your business. In short, separate finances mean smoother sailing for your enterprise!*"

Alex read it through. It was a bit longer than he might have written, but the tone was indeed friendly and it covered all the points: clear records, easier taxes, legal protection. He made a couple of manual tweaks, shortening a sentence and swapping out "smoother sailing" (maybe too colloquial for some clients) with "fewer headaches." Overall, it was excellent. What might have taken him half an hour of pondering and wordsmithing had been generated in moments.

He saved the edited tip in the draft newsletter document and crossed that task off his list with a satisfied check mark. *Alright, what next?*

Encouraged, Alex decided to use ChatGPT for a more complex task: brainstorming ideas for a client. One of his clients, a small manufacturing company, had seen profit margins shrinking, and the client had asked for suggestions on improving profitability. Alex had a meeting with them later in the week and planned to propose a few strategies. He already had some ideas based on his experience, like negotiating better material costs and optimizing their product mix, but it wouldn't hurt to see if the AI could generate any additional suggestions he hadn't considered.

He typed a question without much detail: "How can a company improve its profit margins?"

The answer came quickly, but it was very general:

ChatGPT: *"A company can improve its profit margins by either increasing revenue or reducing costs. Strategies might include raising prices (if the market will tolerate it), increasing sales volume through marketing, cutting unnecessary expenses, improving operational efficiency, automating processes to save labor costs, negotiating better deals with suppliers, and focusing on higher-margin products or services. It's also important to reduce waste and improve productivity. Ultimately, the key is to boost each sale's profitability and eliminate inefficiencies."*

Alex frowned slightly. This was all sound advice, but it was the kind of generic answer you'd find in any basic business textbook. It wasn't tailored to the specific situation of his client's manufacturing business facing rising raw material costs. He realized his prompt had been too broad. This was a perfect example of the "garbage in, garbage out" principle, if he asked a vague question, he'd get a vague answer. *Alright, let's try that again with more context.*

He refined his query: "How can a small manufacturing company improve profit margins when raw material costs are rising? Provide specific strategies."

This time, the response was far more insightful:

ChatGPT: *"When a small manufacturing company faces rising raw material costs, it can take several targeted steps to protect and improve profit margins. First, consider optimizing your supply chain: shop around for alternative suppliers or negotiate bulk purchasing contracts to get better rates on materials. Second, look at improving production efficiency: reduce waste and scrap, streamline processes, or invest in equipment that uses materials more efficiently to get more output from the same input. Third, explore product design adjustments: if possible, redesign products to use less of the costliest materials or substitute with more affordable materials without compromising quality. Additionally, you might adjust pricing strategically: raise prices gradually or add a surcharge to partially offset material cost increases, while clearly communicating the reason to customers. Another approach is to focus on high-margin products: direct sales efforts towards products that are less material-cost intensive or have better margins, to balance out the increased costs on other items. Internally, work on overhead cost control: find savings in energy use, maintenance, or labor overtime to compensate for the higher material expense. By combining these strategies, tackling costs, refining pricing, and improving efficiency, a manufacturing firm can cushion the impact of rising material costs and maintain healthier profit margins."*

Alex broke into a grin. This answer was rich with actionable ideas, many of which aligned with his own thoughts but were articulated clearly and with specifics. It mentioned negotiating with suppliers, reducing waste, tweaking product design, focusing on higher-margin products, all excellent points. It even touched on raising prices carefully, something he had been debating suggesting to the client.

He took notes, merging the AI's suggestions with his own. In his meeting prep document, he now had a robust list of strategies to discuss with the client. He felt a surge of confidence, this was like having a knowledgeable colleague to brainstorm with. And it had taught him an important lesson: the quality of the output depended on the quality of his input. When he provided context and specifics in his prompt, ChatGPT gave back far more useful responses.

Better prompting = better answers

Be specific when asking ChatGPT.

That little principle was now clear as day, and he jotted it in his notebook quickly, wanting to remember it.

Later that morning, as the office filled with the usual bustle, Alex continued experimenting in small ways. He had a routine task of reviewing a client's draft financial statements for any obvious issues. Instead of doing it entirely alone, he tried something clever: he pasted one section of the financial statement notes (with any identifying details anonymized) into ChatGPT and asked, "What potential errors or issues should I look for in the above financial statement note about revenue recognition?"

This was a bit of a stunt, he knew, AI couldn't really *know* if the numbers were wrong or if anything was omitted, but it might point out general things to check for. Sure enough, ChatGPT responded with a bullet-pointed list of generic but useful reminders: check that the revenue recognition policy aligns with accounting standards, ensure consistency of figures with the main statements, verify that any deferred revenue is properly classified, etc. It wasn't spotting actual errors in the text he provided (as expected, since that required knowing the context and numbers), but it gave a review checklist that was handy. It was like asking an experienced accountant, "hey, when you read a revenue note, what do you look out for?"

Alex used that checklist to systematically go through the note and the statements. In doing so, he did catch a small inconsistency the client had in their draft: the revenue note described recognizing revenue "when shipped to customers," but the accounts had an entry for goods that were shipped after year-end erroneously included. He might have caught that on his own, but having the AI's prompt to double-check such things made him extra vigilant. It felt like he and the AI together formed a more thorough review team.

Not everything was perfect, of course. Around mid-day, Alex encountered one of ChatGPT's limitations. He was working on a spreadsheet analysis, projecting a client's cash flow for different scenarios. On a whim, he tried feeding a simplified version of the problem into ChatGPT: "If a company has $50,000 cash now, and expects to receive $20,000 each month for the next three months, but needs to pay $30,000 in expenses each month for the next three months, what will its cash balance be at the end of three months?"

He expected the answer to be straightforward: starting 50k, each month +20k -30k yields a net -10k per month, over 3 months that's -30k, so end would be $20,000. To his surprise, ChatGPT's answer came back muddled. It mentioned something about cumulative cash and gave an answer that was not clearly $20,000. It wasn't completely off, but the explanation was confusing and it seemed to double-count some flows. Alex realized that while ChatGPT could handle arithmetic in many cases, it wasn't a spreadsheet. It might have gotten tangled in the phrasing, or perhaps he phrased the problem poorly.

He reworded the question more clearly: "Start with $50k. Each month, cash increases by $20k (inflows) and decreases by $30k (outflows). After 3 months, what is ending cash?" This time the AI answered correctly: $20k, with a clear explanation.

This little incident was a reminder: sometimes the AI might misinterpret or make a mistake, especially if the prompt isn't crystal clear. And occasionally, even if the prompt is clear, it might just err. He recalled reading an online comment about these AI tools sometimes "hallucinating" answers that sounded confident but were wrong. Indeed, one of his coworkers had joked about asking ChatGPT to solve a math puzzle and getting a very authoritative yet incorrect answer. It reinforced Alex's resolve that he should always double-check important outputs himself. The AI was a tool, not an oracle.

Late in the morning, Alex took a break to refill his coffee. In the break area, he found Jason and their older colleague Robert in the middle of a discussion, more like a friendly debate, about, unsurprisingly, AI.

"It's just a fancy autocomplete on steroids," Robert was saying as he stirred creamer into his coffee. Robert had been with the firm for over 35 years and was eyeing retirement in a couple more. He was respected for his deep knowledge and meticulous work, but everyone knew he was not a fan of new software, he still printed out emails to read them. "I don't see how this Chat whatever is going to change my day-to-day. Our work relies on judgment and trust, not some computer spitting out answers."

Jason leaned against the counter, ever the tech advocate. "I get it, you're skeptical. But have you tried it? I used ChatGPT last week to help me draft a proposal for a new client. Saved me at least an hour of time in writing and researching. And it wasn't just spewing random stuff, it gave me a solid starting point that I refined."

Robert grunted. "Maybe for writing fluff. But can it do *real* accounting? Double-check a balance sheet? Find fraud? I doubt it."

Alex jumped in, recalling his own mixed results. "It's not a magic wand, for sure. But it can be useful in certain tasks. I was able to summarize a new accounting standard in plain language pretty quickly using it."

Robert raised an eyebrow. "And was it accurate?"

"I verified it against the source. It was accurate, just condensed," Alex replied. "Of course, I wouldn't use it blindly without checking." He took a sip of his coffee. "I see it as a tool, like when Excel came along. We still needed to know what formulas to use, but it sure made calculations faster."

Robert sighed, a hint of a smile on his face. "I remember when Excel was new. Some old-timers swore they'd never give up their ledger books." He shook his head, conceding the point. "Turned out, you either learned Excel or you got left behind."

"Exactly," Jason said. "I think this AI is similar. No one's saying it replaces us. It just *augments* what we do."

Robert shrugged. "We'll see. I'll keep an open mind... somewhat. But I worry about quality control. If folks start leaning on it too much, errors could slip through. And what about confidentiality? We handle sensitive client data, can't just be typing that into some website."

"That's a valid concern," Alex admitted. He had been careful not to input anything confidential. "I haven't put any client names or numbers in there, just generic scenarios. Until we know about data privacy, it's better to be cautious."

Jason nodded. "True, we should be careful. The basic version of ChatGPT isn't specifically secure for financial data. There are enterprise versions that promise privacy, but they cost money. I heard big firms are making deals to use these tools internally. Maybe that's something our firm will consider if the partners get on board."

Robert chuckled. "Ha! I bet the partners are more interested in anything that can make us work faster, whether we like it or not. Why do you think we're having that meeting on Friday? They want to squeeze more productivity out of us." He finished stirring his coffee and took a careful sip. "I just hope they don't expect me to become a computer wizard in my final years here."

Alex offered a reassuring smile. "If they do bring in new tools, I'm sure we'll get training. And we'll help each other out. You taught me half of what I know about auditing, Robert. The least I can do is show you how to talk to a chatbot, if it comes to that."

Robert laughed, the lines around his eyes crinkling. "Fair enough, Alex. If I must converse with the little robot, I'll come find you." With that, he gave a mock salute and headed back to his desk.

When Jason and Alex were alone, Jason said under his breath, "I get where he's coming from. Change is hard. But I'm glad you're giving this a try, Alex. A few of us younger folks were worried you'd be in the 'no-AI' camp."

Alex shook his head. "I admit, I was nervous at first. Still am, a bit. But after dipping my toe in, I see the benefits. I just want to make sure I use it correctly."

Jason raised his coffee cup. "To using it correctly, then."

Alex clinked his mug against Jason's. "Hear, hear."

Back at his desk, Alex reflected on that exchange. Robert's points about quality control and confidentiality were important. He made a note to himself to find out whether the firm had any policy on using AI tools. It hadn't been mentioned yet, but perhaps it would come up at Friday's meeting. In the meantime, he would stay cautious: only general questions, no client specifics.

As he looked over the morning's work and felt a growing sense of accomplishment. By experimenting carefully, he had already integrated AI into a few workflows: writing, brainstorming, summarizing, even reviewing. It wasn't perfect and he had to remain vigilant for errors. But he'd discovered a multifaceted power tool where before he'd only had hand tools. The trick was learning the right way to wield it.

He updated his notebook with his observations:

> Be careful with generic questions, add context for useful answers.
>
> Always double-check AI outputs. Trust, but verify every detail.

Those notes joined the others he had written, gradually forming a mini-playbook for himself on how to adapt to this new working companion.

As lunchtime arrived, Alex felt something he hadn't in a while on a workday: a spark of excitement. The initial trials and errors were teaching him not just about ChatGPT's capabilities, but also about his own ability to adapt and learn. The fear of being left behind was starting to give way to the thrill of getting ahead.

Chapter 4: Separating Myth from Reality

That evening, with his daughter busy on her homework and Maria catching up on a favorite show, Alex found some quiet time to dig deeper into the world that had so suddenly shaken up his own: the world of AI in accounting. The conversations at work had left him curious. He didn't just want to rely on Jason's enthusiasm or Robert's skepticism; he wanted facts. If he was going to truly adapt, he needed to understand the current state of research and the trends shaping his profession.

He opened his laptop on the dining table so he could spread out a few printed articles as well. A flood of online headlines appeared as he searched:

> "Accountants Embracing AI, Saving Hours Each Week"
>
> "Will AI Take Accounting Jobs? Experts Weigh In."
>
> "Big Four Firms Investing Billions in AI Technologies."
>
> "Future of Jobs Report: The Impact of Automation on White-Collar Roles."

He clicked on a piece from *Accounting Today* that looked relevant. It cited a recent poll of accountants in the U.S. and U.K. The findings surprised him: 59% of accountants said they already use AI in their work, well above the average of other professions. Alex raised his eyebrows at that. More than half? He hadn't realized adoption had gotten that far.

What really caught his attention was how much time these early adopters *said* they were saving. The survey reported that some accountants were saving up to 30 hours per week on certain repeatable, manual tasks, things like data entry, reconciliations, drafting emails, or preparing standard summaries. Alex read that line twice. Thirty hours sounded enormous. But the article clarified that this figure reflected the upper range of what was possible, not the typical experience for everyone.

Still, even if AI saved a few hours a week, or even one or two hours a day, that was meaningful. The takeaway wasn't that accountants would suddenly only work ten hours a week. It was that the right tools, used the right way, could meaningfully reduce drudge work and free up time for higher-value work.

Alex sat back, absorbing that. If true, it meant that those who leveraged AI effectively were dramatically boosting their efficiency. No wonder Jason seemed so upbeat; maybe he was already among that 59%. Alex couldn't help but wonder what tasks those respondents were automating to reclaim so much time. The article listed common uses: data entry, summarizing information, generating documents, even making recommendations or answering voice queries. It sounded exactly like the things he had begun exploring in the past two days.

He jotted in his notebook:

> Majority of accountants using AI; huge time savings (30+ hrs/week).

The next part of the article struck a chord with him and echoed Robert's concerns. It said that despite the enthusiasm, many accountants were wary of trusting AI for certain tasks. According to the survey, only about half trusted AI with tasks like research or fact-checking, and fewer trusted it with tasks like creating client deliverables or regulatory reports. A notable chunk, 12%, didn't trust AI to handle anything important at all. And 70% of accountants felt AI was advancing too quickly for comfort, a higher percentage than professionals in other industries. That gave Alex pause. He certainly sympathized with the feeling, things *were* moving fast. Yesterday's science fiction was today's reality, or so it seemed.

He added another note:

> Trust issues: many don't fully trust AI outputs yet; concern about rapid pace (70% say too fast).

That was a reminder that while early adopters were diving in, plenty of others were pumping the brakes, much like Robert.

Alex clicked on another link, this one a blog post on a professional accounting site addressing the question on everyone's mind: *Will AI replace accounting jobs?* The author cited the World Economic Forum's 2025 Future of Jobs Report, which predicted that roles like accounting, bookkeeping, and payroll clerks could see significant declines in the coming years due to AI and automation. In fact, those roles were listed among the top ten declining job categories globally. Reading that made Alex swallow hard, there it was in black and white, a prestigious organization essentially warning that some accounting jobs might go the way of the dodo. It was a sobering forecast, and a year ago he might have panicked seeing that.

But the article didn't stop at the dire prediction. It went on to say that the real impact of AI on jobs was complex and likely to unfold over many years, not overnight. Experts argued that worrying about AI "taking jobs" could be alleviated by understanding what tasks these tools could and could not do. The nuance was that AI would eliminate or automate certain tasks, especially the more routine, repetitive ones, but that didn't automatically translate to entire jobs vanishing in one swoop.

A quote from the piece resonated: *"I can think of few professions that have disappeared because of a new technology,"* one accounting professor said, noting how people predicted the end of accountants with the advent of computers, spreadsheets, and other tech, yet the profession endured. Professions change and adapt, he emphasized, rather than simply getting obliterated overnight. That perspective made Alex feel a bit more at ease. After all, he had lived through the rise of powerful accounting software, and rather than replace him, those tools had just become part of his everyday work.

The article also made a point that gave Alex a spark of optimism: the fastest-growing skill in demand for accountants was proficiency with AI and big data. Some firms were already factoring AI skills into their hiring decisions. In other words, those who could wield these new tools were becoming more valuable, not less. Embracing AI could be a career boost, whereas shunning it might actually be the bigger risk.

Alex scribbled:

> Jobs evolving, not gone. Faster to adapt = more marketable. Learn AI = future-proof skill.

He continued reading through a few more sources. One news report described how a Big Four firm, PwC, was investing heavily, over $1 billion, to integrate AI into its services and train its staff. They were even rolling out a version of ChatGPT for all their employees, with custom AI models to help with tasks like tax return review and report generation. It occurred to Alex that if giants like PwC were betting big on AI, it would inevitably filter down through the entire industry. His own mid-sized firm might not have that level of resources, but eventually, clients would expect the same efficiency and insight that those advanced tools could provide. And firms that failed to keep up would lose business to those that did.

Finally, Alex opened an article that directly addressed the emotional side of this transition. It talked about the *"uncomfortable disruptive phase"* that workers might go through as AI becomes more prevalent, but predicted that once people adjusted, they would actually be happier for it. The logic was that AI could take over the drudgery, the boring, repetitive grind that no one really enjoyed, freeing people to focus on more interesting and fulfilling parts of their jobs. One expert was quoted saying, *"If ChatGPT and other technologies can remove the 'boring' stuff, everyone is better off,"* and that the work gets done more efficiently and effectively, with the worker able to focus on more enjoyable parts of their work. That struck a chord. Alex thought of the hours he'd spent in past years doing tedious cross-checks or data cleanup. If those hours had been fewer, and instead he could have spent more time advising clients or devising strategies, he certainly would have found the work more rewarding.

He also noted a candid admission in that piece: there would indeed be a period of disruption and discomfort as roles shifted and people learned to work alongside AI. But after that adjustment, the expert believed, people would likely wonder how they ever lived without these tools, just as they now couldn't imagine doing everything manually that software now handles.

By the time Alex finished his impromptu research session, he had filled a page in his notebook with key points and quotes. He drew a line at the bottom and summarized in his own words what he'd learned:

> AI adoption is already significant in accounting and growing fast. Many accountants report huge time savings, using AI for data entry, summarizing, drafting documents, and more.
>
> People are divided on trust. There's excitement about efficiency, but also caution, many don't trust AI for high-stakes tasks yet and feel things are moving very quickly.
>
> Jobs vs Tasks: AI will automate tasks, especially routine ones, but likely won't eliminate accountants wholesale. Roles will shift towards oversight, analysis, and advisory work, with repetitive work handled by AI.

Adaptation is key: Those who learn to use AI become more valuable and have an edge. AI skills are in demand, and firms are investing in upskilling their workforce to use these tools.

Quality of work-life could improve: By taking away drudgery, AI might let accountants focus on more interesting work, potentially improving job satisfaction (after the initial adjustment phase).

Continuous learning needed: The technology will keep evolving, so ongoing learning and adaptation will be part of the job, much like keeping up with new accounting standards, now one must keep up with new tech as well.

Alex capped his pen, feeling a sense of clarity. The fog of uncertainty was lifting, replaced by a more nuanced understanding. Yes, there were risks and unknowns, but there were also opportunities, big ones. The narrative wasn't simply "AI comes, accountants go." It was more like "Accountants who leverage AI will thrive, and those who don't may struggle."

Importantly, he realized, attitude mattered. Fear of the unknown could paralyze him or make him resistant, whereas embracing a learning mindset could turn AI into an asset rather than a threat. In that moment, Alex made a decision: he was going to lean in and become the kind of accountant who leverages these new tools, not the kind who hopes they'll just go away.

He glanced at the calendar on his phone. Tomorrow was Wednesday; the big staff meeting was on Friday. He had a couple of days before then. With the knowledge he'd gained tonight, he actually felt eager for that meeting. Instead of dreading it, he was now curious what the firm's leadership would say. Would they announce new AI initiatives? Training? Or simply encourage everyone to experiment? Whatever the case, Alex felt he could contribute meaningfully to that conversation now, maybe even share some of his early successes and the facts he'd gathered.

Before shutting down his laptop, Alex couldn't resist one more quick interaction with the tool that had sparked this journey. He opened the ChatGPT window and typed: "Give me one sentence of advice for an accountant adapting to AI."

The response was almost instant, as usual, and right on point. He smiled and copied that line into his notebook. It neatly encapsulated everything he'd come to realize.

> Embrace AI as your assistant, not your replacement, and focus on learning how it can augment your skills to deliver even more value.

With a lighter heart, Alex closed his laptop. The myths and exaggerated fears had been weighed against facts and expert insights, and reality looked far more manageable, and even exciting, than the nightmare scenarios he'd imagined a few days ago. Armed with information and a plan to keep learning, he felt ready to continue his journey of adaptation with a lot more confidence.

Chapter 5: New Skills and Tools

By Wednesday, Alex felt like a different person from the nervous accountant who had read that frightening headline on Monday. Armed with both hands-on practice and solid research, he was more confident and adventurous in his approach to AI. It showed in the way he tackled his work that day, with a mix of curiosity and creativity that he hadn't felt in years.

One of the first things he did that morning was share a bit of his new knowledge with a few colleagues. In an email thread about Friday's upcoming staff meeting, someone had jokingly posted a meme of a robot wearing a suit and tie, with the caption "I'm here to audit you." The lighthearted banter opened the door, and Alex replied to the group with a short note:

"Interesting times! FYI, saw a stat that ~59% of accountants are already using AI tools in some way. Also read that it's sometimes saving some folks up to 30 hours a week of repetitive work. Crazy, right? I've been testing ChatGPT myself on small tasks (summaries, draft emails) and it's been surprisingly helpful. Looking forward to discussing more on Friday."

He kept the tone casual, but he wanted to signal to his peers that AI wasn't just a sci-fi concept, it was here, and it could be a boon. A couple of junior staff quickly replied with excitement, "Yes! I've used it to generate code snippets for Excel, super useful!" wrote one, while others reacted with thumbs-up emojis. Robert, unsurprisingly, did not respond in the thread, but Alex noticed him peering curiously at Alex's screen later; perhaps even the skeptics were starting to pay attention.

Throughout the day, Alex continued to "level up" his AI skills with new experiments:

Voice Interaction: In the late morning, while taking a short break, Alex decided to try the voice input feature of ChatGPT on his phone. He opened the mobile app and, instead of typing, he tapped the microphone icon. Quietly, he asked, "What are some quick ways to analyze a spreadsheet for unusual data points?" speaking just as he would to a virtual assistant. The app recorded his question and, within moments, ChatGPT was listing suggestions on his phone screen: using filters to find outliers, sorting columns to spot extremes, applying conditional formatting to highlight anomalies, and so on. Reading the answer, Alex realized he often did those things instinctively, but seeing them listed step-by-step was like a ready checklist he could share with a junior staffer. The voice recognition had worked flawlessly, it was convenient to just speak and get a written response. *Good to know,* he thought. If his hands were ever full or he was on the go, he could query AI without even typing.

Excel Formula Wizardry: Just before lunch, Alex encountered a minor task that had always irked him. He had a spreadsheet of client addresses, and he needed to extract the first word of each client's city name (a weird request from a marketing team that wanted to group cities by first letter, for some reason). There were dozens of entries. In the past, he might try to remember an Excel formula or, more likely, manually copy-paste using Text-to-Columns or some clunky method. Instead, he decided to ask ChatGPT for the formula. He typed: "Excel formula to extract the first word from a cell's text."

The AI responded instantly with a formula using Excel's functions:

"Use the formula:

=IFERROR(LEFT(A1, FIND(" " , A1 & " ") - 1), A1)

This will give you the first word in cell A1. It works by finding the position of the first space and extracting everything to the left of it. The IFERROR part handles cells with only one word (no spaces). Copy this formula down for other cells, changing A1 to the cell reference as needed."

Alex copied the formula from the response, adjusted the cell reference to the appropriate column in his sheet, and voilà, it worked perfectly, extracting the first word of each city name in an instant. He couldn't help but do a little triumphant finger tap on his desk. What might have taken him 10-15 minutes of fiddling (or searching online for the right formula) had been solved in seconds.

He reflected how this one tiny win exemplified something larger: *AI didn't replace my work; it replaced the tedious figuring out of the tool, letting me apply the solution faster.* He still needed to know what he wanted (the first word of the city), but he didn't need to memorize every Excel trick in the book, ChatGPT had become a quick reference guide, a technical assistant.

He documented this in his notebook too, with a bit of humor:

> ChatGPT = my new "tech support" for Excel magic.

Learning Through Teaching: In the afternoon, an opportunity arose to cement his own understanding by teaching others. One of the newer hires, a recent college grad named Priya, was struggling with drafting a letter to a client explaining a complex tax reconciliation. She came by Alex's desk looking flustered and asked if he had time to help review her draft. Alex remembered how ChatGPT had helped him draft a similar message and saw a chance to both help her and introduce her to a new tool.

He looked over her draft first, giving some pointers on tone and clarity. Then he gently asked, "Have you tried using any AI tools to help with stuff like this? Like ChatGPT?"

She shook her head, "I've heard of it, but I haven't really used it. I wasn't sure if we're allowed or if it's any good for professional writing."

"Well, let's see an example," Alex said. He was mindful not to push too hard, some folks might take it as criticism of their writing, but Priya seemed genuinely interested. They sat together at his computer. "Let's feed it a basic prompt about what we need. Nothing confidential, just the scenario."

He typed into ChatGPT: "Draft a concise, polite letter explaining a discrepancy found in a tax reconciliation, and assuring the client it will be resolved."

ChatGPT produced a solid, general template of a letter. Alex and Priya read it together. It said things like, "We discovered a discrepancy in the tax reconciliation for your account... we are actively investigating... we will adjust the records and ensure accuracy... we apologize for any inconvenience..." and so on, in a professional tone.

Priya's eyes widened a bit. "That's actually really helpful. It's like 90% there."

"Exactly," Alex smiled. "Now, you wouldn't send it as-is. But you can use it to compare with your draft and see if there are phrases or structure you find useful." They spent a few minutes aligning her draft more closely with the AI-suggested structure, while keeping specifics that applied to the client's case.

"This is a game-changer," she said, clearly relieved to have the letter almost ready to go. "I was stuck on how to phrase things without sounding accusatory. This gave me a neutral, professional tone to work from."

After she left, Alex felt a warm sense of satisfaction. In helping a colleague, he had reinforced his own learning. Teaching someone else how to use the tool responsibly (in this case, by using generic information and then customizing the output) also made him think more about guidelines for himself. He recalled from his research that confidentiality was paramount. Even though they used a generic prompt, he still reminded Priya to be cautious about inputting any client-identifying data into the AI. She agreed wholeheartedly, making a note to herself.

Approaching Complexity: By late afternoon, Alex felt ready to tackle something more ambitious. A client had provided a dataset of expenses and revenues broken down by product line and region, and he needed to analyze it for trends and outliers to discuss in a meeting next week. It was a lot of data, something he would normally dump into Excel PivotTables and spend a few hours slicing and dicing.

He decided to see how ChatGPT might assist in analysis. Of course, he wasn't about to upload the raw data (both for confidentiality and sheer volume reasons), but he tried a different approach: asking for a strategy. He described the scenario in general terms to ChatGPT: "I have a dataset of revenues and expenses for multiple product lines across several regions for the past year. What's a good approach to identify key trends and any outliers or anomalies in this data?"

The AI responded with a systematic approach:

1. Summarize overall performance by product line and region to see big-picture trends (which product lines or regions are most profitable or have biggest expenses).

2. Look at trends over time (are certain months or quarters spiking or dipping notably for some categories?).

3. Calculate profit margins for each product line and region to see if some are significantly higher or lower than others.

4. Use visualization (maybe make a simple chart) to highlight any outlier values (like a bar chart for each product line's profit, or a time series line graph for each region).

5. Investigate any anomalies (for example, if one region's expenses spiked in one quarter, dig into why, perhaps an operational issue or one-time event).

Reading this, Alex felt a bit like he was reviewing advice from a mentor or a textbook distilled into practical steps. These were all things he could do, nothing novel individually, but having the structured plan written out was helpful. It was like a checklist to make sure he didn't forget any angle of analysis.

He followed the AI's suggested steps methodically using Excel and a visualization tool they had. Sure enough, he identified a couple of interesting insights: one product line's expenses jumped in Q3 (which upon investigation corresponded to a temporary spike in raw material prices, something he made a note to explain to the client), and one region had consistently lower profit margins than others (pointing perhaps to higher fixed costs there, worth exploring).

By leaning on the AI for a planning perspective, Alex felt he had been more thorough and quicker in his analysis prep. It was like brainstorming with a colleague who had a bird's-eye view, ensuring he examined the data from multiple angles.

As the workday wound down, Alex organized his notes for the client analysis and tidied up his desk. It had been another productive day, arguably more productive than usual, thanks to his growing repertoire of AI-augmented skills. He realized that in the span of just a few days, he had evolved from viewing AI as a threat to treating it as a multifaceted tool:

- A writing assistant for drafting and refining communications.
- A research assistant for quick facts, formulas, and methods.
- A brainstorming partner for analytical approaches and strategy.
- A tutor/mentor at his fingertips for learning new tricks (like Excel formulas or summarizing new topics).

No wonder those survey respondents reported so much time saved. Alex could already feel the difference. And with that extra efficiency came a surprising benefit: he was less stressed.

Tasks that he might have procrastinated on (dreading the tedium or the writer's block associated with them) were getting done faster, almost effortlessly. He even noticed he'd barely touched his usual afternoon coffee, he simply hadn't felt the sluggish slump that normally came from mental fatigue.

Before leaving, he scribbled one more note to himself on a sticky and stuck it on his monitor:

"AI can't do my job, but it can sure help me do my job better."

It was a thought worth keeping front and center, especially with the staff meeting coming up. He anticipated AI would be a hot topic, and he felt ready to contribute. More than that, he felt ready to keep learning, keep experimenting, and keep pushing the boundaries of how he could integrate AI into his professional toolkit.

As he grabbed his bag and headed out, Alex thought about how much had changed in just a few days. The core of his work, helping clients, analyzing numbers, solving problems, was still the same. But the way he went about it was transforming, becoming more efficient and innovative. Far from feeling devalued, he felt *empowered.* And that was perhaps the biggest surprise of all in this journey of adapting with AI.

Chapter 6: Helping a Friend

On Wednesday evening, after his daughter Sophie had retreated to her room for homework, Alex picked up his phone to call his friend Mark. They hadn't spoken in a couple of weeks, and Alex was eager to share some of his newfound hope and perhaps lend Mark a hand. The phone rang several times before Mark answered.

Mark's voice was tired. "Hey Alex."

"Hey, how are you holding up?" Alex asked gently.

Mark sighed. "I'm… I'm okay, I guess. Been better. I'm sending out resumes left and right, but not getting much response. It's tough out there."

Alex could hear the discouragement. Losing a job was a blow that could rattle anyone's confidence. Mark had always been hardworking and loyal to his company, but he hadn't needed to job-hunt in nearly a decade. The whole process had changed dramatically, even more so with the pandemic years and now new tech on the scene.

"I was thinking," Alex began, "maybe I could swing by or we could meet up and go over your resume and stuff together. Two heads better than one?"

There was a pause, and then Mark said quietly, "You'd do that? I… I'd really appreciate it, man. I feel like I'm shooting in the dark here."

"Of course. How about tomorrow after work? We can grab coffee or I can come to your place."

They settled on meeting at Mark's apartment the next evening.

Thursday after work, Alex arrived at Mark's place with his laptop and a positive mindset. Mark greeted him at the door wearing a faded t-shirt and jeans, looking a bit unkempt, the look of someone who'd been spending a lot of days alone at home. Still, he managed a grateful smile for Alex.

They sat at the small dining table that Mark had converted into a makeshift job-hunting station, cluttered with printouts of job listings and a notebook of scribbled applications sent. Alex noticed a copy of Mark's resume and cover letter among the papers.

"Alright," Alex said, rolling up his sleeves figuratively. "Let's see what we're working with."

They spent the first twenty minutes reviewing Mark's current resume. Mark had been a Back Office Operations Manager at the bank, handling things like transaction processing, compliance checks, and system improvements. His resume listed his duties, but in a rather generic way. Alex remembered something he'd learned from a career counselor long ago: resumes should focus on accomplishments, not just responsibilities.

"Your resume should brag a little," Alex said. "Right now it's saying what you did, but not how well you did it or what impact you had."

Mark rubbed his face. "I know… I've never been good at that. I hate 'selling' myself. I just do my job."

"I hear you. But think of it as telling your story. Let's identify a couple of your big wins at the bank. Like here, " Alex pointed at a bullet: "Implemented new reconciliation system." "What did that achieve?"

Mark thought. "It… well, it reduced errors, and saved time."

"How much reduction? Any idea?"

"I think errors dropped by like 30% after we rolled it out. And the team probably saved a few hours each week on manual corrections."

"Those are solid numbers. Let's include them."

Now, instead of just manually rewriting the bullet, Alex had an idea. He opened his laptop and said, "I've been using this tool called ChatGPT. It's like an AI assistant. Let's feed it some details about that project and see if it can help us phrase it strongly."

Mark looked skeptical. "AI… like that thing that writes essays? How's that gonna help my resume?"

"Trust me, it can help with wording. We'll use your facts, just make it sound sharp."

He logged into ChatGPT and typed: "Rewrite the following resume bullet to emphasize achievements: 'Implemented a new reconciliation system for transaction processing, which reduced errors by 30% and saved 5 hours per week in manual work.'"

ChatGPT quickly responded with a punchier version: *"Implemented a new transaction reconciliation system that cut processing errors by 30% and saved 5 hours per week in manual corrections, significantly improving operational efficiency."*

"Wow," Mark said, reading it. "That does sound better."

"Right? It's basically what you just told me, but polished." Alex grinned. He inserted that bullet into Mark's resume draft.

They proceeded through the rest of Mark's resume, point by point. For areas where Mark struggled to articulate his contributions, Alex would ask him guiding questions and then use ChatGPT to help shape the language.

For example, Mark had also overseen a team of 8 people. His original resume said: "Managed a team of 8." Alex asked what that entailed. Mark explained he trained new hires and redistributed workloads to improve turnaround time on certain processes. They turned that into a bullet like: *"Managed and trained a team of 8, improving transaction processing turnaround by streamlining task allocation and mentorship."* Again, Alex had enlisted ChatGPT to tighten the phrasing, and then they tweaked it to be accurate.

With each improved bullet, Mark's expression brightened a bit. His resume was transforming from a bland list into a results-focused document showcasing his value.

Next up was the summary at the top of the resume. Mark's current one-line summary was very generic. Alex suggested they create a stronger professional summary that highlighted Mark's experience and skills. They tried a prompt: "Write a professional profile summary for a resume of an operations manager with 10+ years in banking, specializing in process improvement, compliance, and team leadership."

ChatGPT produced: *"Operations Manager with 10+ years in the banking industry, adept at streamlining processes, ensuring compliance, and leading teams to exceed performance targets. Proven track record of reducing errors and improving efficiency, with strong expertise in back-office operations and regulatory compliance. Recognized for effective leadership and strategic improvements that drive productivity and accuracy."*

Mark let out a low whistle. "Where was this thing when I was struggling with that summary last week? This sounds like someone I'd hire."

Alex chuckled. "It does paint a nice picture. Let's make sure it's all true." They tweaked one or two phrases to better fit Mark's voice (for instance, Mark was uncomfortable claiming "exceed performance targets" without specifics, so they toned that down). The final summary still read powerfully.

With the resume looking great, they moved on to the cover letter. Mark had drafted one, but it was a very standard template, essentially a rehash of his resume in paragraph form. Alex knew a cover letter needed to convey enthusiasm and fit for the role, not just repeat resume points.

He suggested using ChatGPT to generate a draft that they could customize. He prompted: "Draft a cover letter for an operations manager position in a bank, highlighting experience in process improvement, compliance, and team leadership. Applicant was laid off due to restructuring and is enthusiastic about contributing to a new company."

ChatGPT's draft was surprisingly empathetic and polished. It started with a nice hook about being excited to apply, mentioned his years of experience, gently noted the layoff as part of structural changes (positioning it as an external event, no fault of performance), and expressed eagerness to bring his skills to deliver similar efficiency gains for the prospective employer.

Mark read through it, nodding slowly. "This is… really good. It's like it knows exactly how to phrase what I wanted to say, without me sounding desperate."

They tailored the draft to insert the actual company name and a few specifics relevant to the job posting Mark was targeting. The result was a cover letter that felt genuine and focused on how Mark's experience would benefit the new employer, rather than just lamenting his layoff or listing his resume points.

By now, Mark was thoroughly impressed. He leaned back and looked at Alex. "I can't believe how much we did in under two hours. I've been agonizing over this stuff for weeks."

Alex smiled and put a hand on his friend's shoulder. "Sometimes you just need the right tools and a fresh perspective. Honestly, I only started using this AI assistant a few days ago. I was skeptical too, but it's been a huge help."

Mark shook his head in disbelief. "I was so worried you'd say I have to learn coding or something complicated. But this… it's like talking to a helpful guide. Why didn't I try this sooner?"

"Don't beat yourself up. A lot of people don't know what these tools can do, or feel weird about using them. But it's becoming common. Heck, I read a statistic that a majority of accountants use AI tools and save tons of time. It's not just accountants either. People in all sorts of jobs are using it to write, to brainstorm, you name it."

Mark looked at the screen thoughtfully. "You think I could use it to practice interviews too? I get so nervous with those."

Alex's face lit up. "Absolutely. We can do that right now."

He prompted ChatGPT: "Pretend you are a hiring manager interviewing a candidate for an operations manager position at a bank. Ask one interview question at a time, then wait for an answer."

The AI responded with a question: *"Can you tell me about a time you implemented a significant process improvement? What was the challenge and what result did you achieve?"*

Alex turned to Mark. "That's a classic question. Go ahead, answer as if we're in an interview. Take your time."

Mark attempted an answer, describing the reconciliation system project. His first try was a bit rambling and heavy on technical details. Alex gently coached him to structure his answer better: situation, action, result. They tried again, and Mark's second attempt was much more concise and impactful: he set the context of needing to reduce errors, explained how he led the implementation of a new system, and ended with the results (30% error reduction, time saved).

ChatGPT then provided feedback when Alex asked for it: "Give feedback on that answer and suggest improvement." The AI responded with a polite critique: it praised the inclusion of a concrete result, and suggested Mark could emphasize his leadership role more or mention any collaboration with IT.

Mark was amazed. "It's like a mock interviewer and coach combined."

They went through a couple more questions with ChatGPT's help:
- "How do you handle tight deadlines or pressure?"
- "Why do you think you're a good fit for this role?"

Each time, Mark practiced answering, and Alex, sometimes with AI's feedback, helped refine his responses.

As they wrapped up, Mark's posture was more upright and his voice more confident. "I actually feel prepared now," he said, sounding almost surprised. "I was dreading getting a call for an interview, but now… I kind of hope I get one soon so I can put this to use."

"You will," Alex assured him. "You're a strong candidate, Mark. Sometimes it's just about presenting yourself in the best light. And you've got that now, a great resume, a solid cover letter, and you're ready to nail the interview."

Mark's eyes grew moist for a second as he closed his laptop. "I can't thank you enough, Alex. I was really in a dark place. You gave me a lifeline here. And this AI thing… I had no idea. Honestly, I was almost resentful of the idea of AI, thinking it took my job. But you showed me it can help me get my next job."

Alex gave a sympathetic smile. "I know that feeling. I was terrified of it at first too. But I've learned that it's more about how we use it. Think of AI as a tool, sometimes even a teammate. It can help us improve, like it did with your resume and practice, but we're still in control."

Mark nodded. "Makes sense. It's like a supercharged Google mixed with a coach. I'm definitely going to keep using it as I apply to more places. Maybe I'll even ask it for career change ideas, since banking is changing so much."

"That's a great idea," Alex said. "Actually, let's do a quick one now. What's a role you've thought about pivoting to?"

Mark pondered. "Maybe something in compliance or risk management. Similar skill set, growing field."

Alex typed: "What are some growing career paths for someone with 10 years of banking operations and compliance experience?"

ChatGPT responded with a list:

"1. Risk Management Specialist, banks and financial institutions need people to identify and mitigate operational risks.

2. Compliance Officer, ensuring organizations meet regulatory requirements (a natural transition from operations with compliance).

3. Financial Technology (FinTech) Operations Manager, leveraging your operations experience in a tech-forward environment.

4. Business Process Consultant, use your expertise to advise companies on improving their back-office processes.

5. Project Manager in Financial Services, managing initiatives like system implementations, which you have experience in."

"Those are some solid leads," Alex said, showing Mark. "Could widen your search to some of these areas too."

Mark breathed in deeply, and for the first time in a while, Alex saw genuine optimism on his friend's face. "I will. This is the most hopeful I've felt since I got laid off. Thank you, Alex. Really."

They stood up and gave each other a quick hug. It had been a productive session, but more importantly, it reminded both of them that with the right support, human and AI, even daunting challenges could be overcome.

As Alex left Mark's apartment that evening, he felt a deep sense of satisfaction. Helping Mark not only lifted his friend's spirits, but it reinforced Alex's own journey. He had gone from needing guidance to providing it, using what he learned about AI to lift someone else up. In doing so, he realized the ripple effect of adapting: it wasn't just about one person surviving change, it was about spreading that empowerment to others.

On the drive home, Alex couldn't help but smile. A week ago, both he and Mark had viewed AI as something that might take away their livelihoods. Now, AI had become a part of the solution in reclaiming confidence and moving forward. If that wasn't a sign of adapting with AI, he didn't know what was.

Chapter 7: Family Matters

Over the weekend, Alex found that his experiences with AI were not only benefiting his work and friends, but could also be a positive force at home. Two particular incidents, one with his daughter and one with his wife, drove home the versatility of this new tool and the importance of using it wisely.

On Saturday afternoon, Alex was in the kitchen preparing a sandwich when he noticed his 16-year-old daughter, Sophie, at the dining table with her laptop open and a rather guilty expression on her face. Scattered around her were notes and a copy of *To Kill a Mockingbird*, which he knew was her English class novel. As a high school junior she was doing well academically and socially and Alex was a proud papa.

"Everything okay, Soph?" he asked, wiping his hands and walking over.

"Mm-hm," Sophie replied a bit too quickly, angling her laptop screen ever so slightly away.

Alex had a hunch what might be going on. He remembered the ongoing discussions among parents about teenagers discovering AI tools. Gently, he probed, "Working on your literature essay?"

She nodded. "It's due Monday. I'm kinda stuck."

Alex pulled out a chair. "Stuck how? Maybe I can help."

Sophie bit her lip, then sighed and turned her laptop so he could see. On the screen was the ChatGPT website with her last prompt still visible: "Write a 5-paragraph book report on To Kill a Mockingbird." The AI had generated a few paragraphs in response.

"I… I just wanted to see what it would do," Sophie said hurriedly. "I'm not going to copy it! But I was so blank on how to start, and, "

Alex raised a hand reassuringly. "Hey, I understand. Tools like this are tempting, especially when you have writer's block. I'm glad you showed me." He read the AI-generated text. It was a competent summary with basic analysis, nothing a million high schoolers hadn't said before, but well-organized.

"The thing is," Alex continued, "using AI like this for an assignment can be risky. Your teacher might have a way to detect if it's AI-written. And more importantly, you wouldn't be flexing your own brain muscles."

Sophie looked down. "I know. It just feels like everyone's using it. Some kids even brag their whole essay was written by ChatGPT and the teacher didn't notice. It's not fair."

Alex understood her frustration. It was a new challenge for education, ensuring students learned and didn't just cheat with AI. "It might seem that way, but trust me, it catches up. And you actually like this book, don't you?"

She nodded. "Yeah, it's pretty good. I just… I'm awful at writing essays."

"Tell you what," Alex said, "let's use ChatGPT in a different way. Not to do the work for you, but to help you do your work."

Sophie looked curious. "Like what?"

"First, let's make sure you really understand what you want to say. How about we have ChatGPT help by asking *you* questions about the book, almost like a mock interviewer? That might get your ideas flowing."

Sophie agreed, and Alex helped her prompt: "Ask me some thought-provoking questions about themes and characters in To Kill a Mockingbird."

ChatGPT responded with a list of questions:

- "What do you think Atticus Finch represents in the novel, and how does he influence Scout's understanding of justice?"
- "How does the setting of Maycomb contribute to the story's central themes of prejudice and empathy?"
- "Can you discuss the importance of the Tom Robinson trial in shaping the moral lessons of the book?"

As Sophie read the questions, she began to talk through answers with Alex. He listened as she articulated her thoughts: how Atticus was a role model of integrity, how the small-town setting magnified biases, how the trial opened Scout's eyes to injustice. Alex occasionally prompted her with "That's a great point, maybe jot that down."

Together, they used ChatGPT in another way: Sophie typed one of her thoughts as a prompt: "Help me outline an essay about how the Tom Robinson trial teaches Scout about justice."

The AI suggested a possible structure: introduction, a paragraph on Scout's innocence at first, a paragraph on the trial events, a paragraph on the aftermath and lessons learned, etc. It provided bullet points rather than full sentences when asked for an outline.

Sophie took those suggestions and said, "Okay, I think I know how to structure it now." She started drafting her essay by herself, referring to the outline and her own notes from their discussion.

Alex reminded her, "Feel free to ask me or even ask ChatGPT if you need to clarify a concept, like, you could ask it to explain what a certain symbol in the book might mean. But the writing and analysis should be yours."

She nodded. After a while of writing, she did have ChatGPT explain the significance of the mockingbird symbol, which she then put into her own words in the essay.

When she finished her draft, Sophie let out a breath of relief. "That was actually easier than I thought, once I had the direction."

"How do you feel about it?" Alex asked.

"Pretty good. I think it's my own voice, just… I needed a push on how to organize my thoughts."

Alex patted her shoulder. "That's exactly the right way to use a tool like this. I'm proud of you. You did the hard part, thinking and writing. The AI just played the tutor."

Sophie gave her dad a quick hug. "Thanks, Dad. I'm glad you didn't just freak out at me."

He smiled. "Believe me, I'm learning too. This stuff is new for everyone. The important thing is: use it to learn, not to cheat. He also pointed out that ChatGPT isn't infallible, it sometimes makes factual mistakes or even "hallucinates" information, so relying on it blindly could backfire academically."

Sophie nodded vigorously. "I won't. I promise." With that, she trotted off to message a friend (likely bragging that her essay was done a whole day early). Alex felt satisfied. He had turned a potential misuse into a teachable moment. And Sophie genuinely engaged with the material rather than copying something.

On Sunday evening, Alex and Maria finally had a bit of quiet time together after dinner. Sophie was in her room, and the two of them sat on the living room couch, each with a mug of tea.

"You've been in such a good mood this week," Maria remarked, tucking her legs under a blanket. "It's a nice change from how stressed you were before."

Alex chuckled. "Yeah, it's been a whirlwind. In a good way. I feel like I'm not fighting the current anymore, you know?"

Maria nodded. She then bit her lip as if deciding whether to say something. "Can I make a confession?"

"Sure."

"Seeing you embrace all these new ideas… it got me thinking about something I've been putting off." She set her mug on the coffee table. "You know how I've always toyed with the idea of selling my handmade candles online?"

Alex's face lit up. He loved her candles, the house often smelled of lavender or vanilla from her experiments. She made beautiful soy candles in decorated glass jars as a hobby and gave them as gifts to friends, who raved about them.

"You absolutely should," he said. "Your candles are amazing. What's been holding you back?"

"A few things," Maria admitted. "I didn't know what to call the business, or how to describe the products in a way that sounds professional. And honestly, marketing isn't my strength. I can design labels and take decent photos, but writing product descriptions or ad copy… I freeze up. It's partly why I never moved forward."

Alex gently took her hand. "What if we tackle some of that right now, together? I have a new assistant who might help." He winked, referring to ChatGPT.

Maria smiled. "You mean the AI? How would that help with… oh! Like brainstorming names or something?"

"Exactly. We can ask it for ideas, and then you pick what resonates."

They opened Alex's laptop on the coffee table so they could both see. Alex typed: "Brainstorm unique, pleasant brand names for a small business selling handmade scented candles."

ChatGPT churned out a list of suggestions:

- "Lumina Aroma"
- "Wick & Whimsy Candles"
- "Ever Glow Crafts"
- "Scented Serenity Co."
- "Aura & Ember"

Maria leaned in, eyes sparkling with interest. "Wick & Whimsy… I kind of like that," she said. "It's cute and hints at candles in a fun way."

"I like it too," Alex agreed. "Let's see a few more options just to be sure." He prompted for more, and ChatGPT gave additional names like "Melted Moonlight," "Cozy Glow Candles," and "Fragrant Haven."

After some back-and-forth, Maria kept coming back to "Wick & Whimsy Candles." "It makes me think of something charming and magical, which is how I want people to feel using my candles," she explained.

"Wick & Whimsy it is," Alex declared, happy to see her excitement building. He made a note of it.

"Now, product descriptions," Maria said. She fetched one of her candles from the shelf, a vanilla lavender blend in a frosted glass jar decorated with pressed flowers. "How would I even begin to describe this eloquently?"

"Let's give it a shot," Alex said, and dictated a prompt as he typed:. "Write a short, charming product description for a handmade lavender vanilla scented soy candle in a decorated glass jar. Emphasize relaxation and artisan craftsmanship."

In seconds, ChatGPT composed a paragraph: "*Unwind with the soothing glow of our Lavender Vanilla Bliss candle. Hand-poured with natural soy wax and infused with pure lavender and warm vanilla, this candle gently fills your space with a calming aroma. Encased in a delicately decorated glass jar adorned with real pressed flowers, each candle is a one-of-a-kind artisan creation. Light this Wick & Whimsy candle to transform any room into a cozy haven of tranquility. Perfect for peaceful evenings or as a thoughtful handmade gift, it's relaxation captured in a jar.*"

Maria placed a hand over her heart in dramatic fashion. "Oh… my… that's lovely!" she exclaimed. "It's like it read my mind and then wrote what I felt but couldn't articulate."

Alex laughed. "It is good. We can tweak any bits if needed, but honestly that's pretty spot on." They changed "Lavender Vanilla Bliss" to "Lavender Vanilla Dream" to match the name she had been thinking of for that scent, but left most of it as-is.

They went on to generate descriptions for two other candles she had in her line (a citrus one and a cinnamon spice one), maintaining a consistent style.

Next, they tackled a short bio for her online shop's About page. Maria prompted, "Write a 2-3 sentence 'About Us' for Wick & Whimsy Candles, a home-based candle studio creating hand-crafted scented candles with natural ingredients, aimed at bringing comfort and whimsy into people's homes."

The AI delivered: "*At Wick & Whimsy Candles, we handcraft each candle with love, natural ingredients, and a touch of magic. What began as a home kitchen experiment blossomed into a passion for creating cozy aromas that spark comfort and whimsy in your home. Every candle is an invitation to slow down, breathe deep, and enjoy a moment of simple joy.*"

Maria gave an approving nod. "That captures my journey and mission perfectly. I might tear up," she joked, wiping an imaginary tear.

Finally, they decided to utilize the AI for a bit of market insight. "Let's roleplay," Alex suggested. "We can have ChatGPT act as a curious customer, so we can anticipate questions."

They prompted: "Imagine you are a customer interested in handmade candles. What are five questions you might ask the seller about the candles or the business?"

ChatGPT listed questions a customer might ask:
1. "What ingredients do you use in your candles? Are they natural and eco-friendly?"

2. "How strong is the scent, and how long does it last when burning?"

3. "Do you make the candles yourself? Can you tell me about your process?"

4. "Is the jar reusable or recyclable after the candle is finished?"

5. "What sets your candles apart from store-bought ones?"

These were great prompts for Maria to think about. She and Alex discussed good answers, many of which Maria already knew by heart but now realized she should highlight, like that she uses 100% soy wax and phthalate-free fragrance oils, that each candle is hand-poured in small batches, and that the pressed flower jars can be repurposed as decorative holders after the candle is done.

"Those Q&As will be perfect for my FAQ section or even social media posts," Maria said, jotting down notes.

In a span of a couple of hours, Maria went from having a nebulous idea to a clear brand name, polished product descriptions, a charming about page, and a strong sense of how to communicate her candles' value. The look of overwhelm she once had when thinking about launching had been replaced with excitement.

"You realize what this means?" Alex said as they started closing up the laptop. "You're officially in business. Wick & Whimsy Candles is happening."

Maria grinned. "It really is, isn't it? I feel like all the pieces I was stuck on are unstuck now. Thank you, Alex."

He shook his head. "Thank *you.* I'm just happy I could help. And thank our AI assistant here, couldn't have done it so quickly otherwise."

Maria gave him a quick kiss on the cheek. "Is it weird that I'm actually looking forward to doing the marketing stuff now? I usually dread it, but seeing these lovely descriptions and knowing I have a 'copywriter' on standby… it's a relief."

"Not weird at all," Alex said. "That's exactly how I've felt this week, tasks I used to dread, I now kind of enjoy, because I have backup. It's like having an intern who never sleeps." He paused. "A very *smart* intern, at that."

They both laughed.

As they got ready for bed that night, Alex reflected on how far things had come in such a short time. His home was now abuzz with the positive ripple effects of embracing AI: Sophie was learning with it (and learning when *not* to lean on it), Maria was launching a dream with its help, and he himself felt more balanced and present, not weighed down by work anxiety as he had been just a week before.

Lying in bed, Maria scrolling through design ideas for her candle labels and Alex mentally preparing for the big work meeting in the morning, Alex felt a warm contentment. Adaptation wasn't just improving his work life; it was enriching his family's life too. He reached over and gave Maria's hand a squeeze. She squeezed back, both of them already dreaming a little easier that night, buoyed by the possibilities the future held.

Chapter 8: Turning Point at the Office

Friday morning arrived, and with it the much-anticipated all-hands staff meeting at McAllister & Lee. Alex walked into the firm's largest conference room feeling a mix of excitement and curiosity. Gone was the dread that had knotted his stomach at the start of the week; now he was eager to see how the leadership would address the topic that had everyone buzzing.

The room filled with about thirty employees, partners, managers, associates, support staff, practically the whole firm. Mr. Morales, the CEO, stood at the front by a projector screen. A slide was displayed titled "Embracing Innovation: AI and The Future of Our Firm." Clearly, they weren't shying away from the subject.

Once everyone settled, Mr. Morales cleared his throat. "Good morning, everyone. I'm sure you've all heard about the rapid developments in artificial intelligence, especially tools like ChatGPT, and how they're starting to impact our industry." A few folks exchanged glances or nods; some, like Jason, smiled knowingly.

Mr. Morales clicked to the next slide, which showed a few statistics. "I want to start with some perspective. A recent industry poll found that nearly 60% of accountants are already using AI at work. Many report significant time savings, on the order of dozens of hours a week, by automating routine tasks." Alex noticed Jason shoot him a quick grin; clearly, those were the same figures Alex had emailed around.

"Now," Mr. Morales continued, "we at McAllister & Lee have always been proud of our personal touch and professional expertise. That doesn't change. But we'd be remiss not to explore technologies that can enhance our efficiency and value to clients. Our goal is to augment our work, not replace the human element."

He then opened the floor briefly. "I'd love to hear if any of you have dabbled with these tools, and what your experiences have been. We're all learning here."

There was a moment of silence. Alex felt his heart thumping, he knew this was an opportunity. After a brief hesitation, he raised his hand.

"Yes, Alex," Mr. Morales acknowledged, looking pleased that someone volunteered.

Taking a breath, Alex stood up so folks could see him. "Well, earlier this week I actually started experimenting with ChatGPT, to be honest because I was concerned about falling behind. And… it's been a game-changer for me, in a good way."

He had everyone's attention now. He briefly described a couple of specific examples: "For instance, I used it to draft a summary of a new tax regulation in plain English for a client. Normally it would take me an hour to carefully word that memo, with the AI's first draft to build on, I finished in 15 minutes. I also had it brainstorm different ways to analyze a large dataset; it gave me a checklist that helped me catch an anomaly I might have missed otherwise."

He saw a few eyebrows raise around the room. Encouraged, he continued, "It's also been great for writing first drafts of emails or reports. Of course, I always review and edit them, it's not perfect, and I'm careful not to feed it sensitive client data, but it's like having a quick assistant to get me started."

When Alex sat down, Jason chimed in next. He shared how he's used ChatGPT to help write a proposal and even to troubleshoot an Excel formula. A couple of other younger staff nodded and added their experiences, one said she used it to practice explaining complex concepts in simpler terms before a client meeting, which helped her confidence.

Not everyone was immediately glowing, though. One of the senior accountants, Linda, folded her arms. "I admit I've been reluctant," she said. "I worry about the accuracy. I mean, if it drafts a memo and gets a number wrong or an interpretation off, that's on us, right? And there's the privacy issue Alex touched on, we have a duty to protect client information."

Mr. Morales nodded solemnly. "Excellent points, Linda. Accuracy and confidentiality are paramount." He looked to the IT director, who was also in the room. "We're investigating secure, enterprise-grade options of these tools. For instance, there are versions of ChatGPT designed for corporate use with encryption and no data retention. If we adopt anything firm-wide, it will be something that addresses confidentiality."

Alex spoke up again gently, building on that. "In the meantime, those of us using the public tool have been careful. I personally either anonymize client data or stick to generic scenarios when using it. And I double-check everything it produces. It's certainly not a 'trust and go' situation, more like a helpful first draft that I then verify and refine." He glanced over at Linda and Robert to make sure they felt heard on that.

Robert scratched his chin and raised a question. "What about the impact on our jobs? I mean, if it saves dozens of hours, does that mean we'll be expected to take on dozens more hours of work? Or fewer of us needed eventually?"

A slight hush fell, it was the blunt question others had probably wondered. Mr. Morales responded candidly, "It's true, AI will make certain tasks faster. But I see that as an opportunity. If routine work takes less time, that frees us up to focus on higher-level analysis, client advisory, and tackling more clients without burning out. Our firm can potentially grow and take on more business with the same staff, or expand our services, rather than reduce staff."

He added with a small smile, "Also, consider the competitive angle. If other firms are leveraging AI to be more efficient and we're not, we could lose business. I'd rather we use it to enhance our work and gain an edge. The human expertise and relationship aspect isn't going away, if anything, it becomes more important."

There were murmurs of agreement around the table. The atmosphere shifted from apprehensive to forward-looking.

Mr. Morales then advanced the slides to a plan outline. "I'm proposing we form a small working group to develop best practices for using AI in our firm's context. This group will experiment, document what works and what doesn't, and help train the rest of the team. We'll address issues like verifying accuracy, maintaining client confidentiality, and integrating AI outputs with our standard workpapers and software."

He scanned the room. "Anyone interested in leading or joining that effort?"

Jason practically shot out of his seat. "Count me in!" he said.

Linda nodded slowly. "I'd like to be part of it, if only to ensure we set proper guidelines and don't cut corners." Her skepticism had turned into a willingness to help shape the process, which Alex found admirable.

After a moment, Alex raised his hand again, a bit more timidly this time. "I'd be willing to lead the group, or co-lead," he offered. "I've already gathered some research on this and started a bit of an internal dialogue." He glanced around and saw several colleagues smiling back; they remembered his email and his comments today.

Mr. Morales broke into a broad grin. "Fantastic. Alex, why don't you take point on this initiative. Work with Jason, Linda, and anyone else who volunteers. I'll allocate some time and budget for you all to test tools, maybe even pilot the enterprise version of ChatGPT or another platform, and attend any trainings you find useful."

Alex felt a flush of pride and responsibility. "I'll do my best," he said, filled with determination.

They spent the rest of the meeting discussing areas where AI could be immediately applied. Ideas flowed:

- The audit team noted they could use AI to quickly summarize lengthy client documents or contracts to identify relevant info.

- The tax team was interested in trying it to double-check logic on complex tax law questions or to generate first drafts of client tax memos (with careful review after).

- Some talked about using it to brainstorm consulting recommendations for clients ("almost like having a silent partner to bounce ideas off," one manager mused).

Alex took copious notes, already envisioning how to organize these experiments.

The meeting wrapped up with a sense of optimism. Mr. Morales ended by saying, "I'm proud of us for confronting this head-on. I truly believe that by adapting, we'll not only protect our relevance but enhance it. Our clients come to us for judgment, insight, and trust, AI is just another tool we can use to deliver those, faster and better."

As people filed out, several colleagues approached Alex. The head of the audit department said, "I'd love to sit with you next week and see what you've been doing with ChatGPT. Maybe it can help with a tedious audit confirmation process we have."

"Absolutely," Alex replied. "Let's schedule a demo session."

Linda gave him a gracious nod. "Thanks for raising those caution points in there. I'm actually intrigued to try it myself now, perhaps you can show me how you used it to summarize that regulation?"

"Of course," Alex said. This was exactly the outcome he'd hoped for, interest tempered with healthy caution, moving forward as a team.

The most unexpected interaction came when Robert shuffled up to him. The older accountant had been quiet after his question, observing the discussion. "Alex," he began, a bit gruffly, "good job in there."

"Thank you, Robert." Alex respected the man greatly, so this meant a lot.

Robert cleared his throat. "Listen, I've been doing things my way a long time. I might need to lean on you as I figure this AI stuff out." It sounded almost like an apology in code.

Alex offered a warm smile. "I'm happy to help, anytime. Maybe we can sit down next week and play around with some examples on a client file you choose. No pressure."

Robert adjusted his spectacles and nodded. "I'd like that. Who knows, maybe these contraptions will help me finally take a proper vacation without lugging a briefcase of papers." He chuckled, and Alex did too.

"Absolutely. If I have my way, we'll all be reclaiming some time," Alex replied.

As Robert left, Jason slapped Alex on the back lightly. "Man, you're like the AI guru of the firm now. I'm psyched to work on this with you."

Alex laughed. "Let's just say 'enthusiast'. Guru might be a stretch, there's so much I'm still learning. But I'm excited. Who would've thought at the start of this week I'd be leading an AI initiative?"

"No one," Jason joked, "least of all you!"

It was true. The transformation in such a short span was almost dizzying. Alex gathered his notes and laptop, feeling a surge of energy. This was a new chapter for the firm, and he was at the helm of it. The fear that had once loomed over him was replaced by a sense of purpose and possibility.

Before heading back to his desk, Alex took a moment to reflect. In the span of days, he had gone from fearing that AI would marginalize his role, to using it to amplify his productivity, to becoming a champion for it within his organization. The technology that threatened to leave him behind had become the catalyst propelling him, and now his firm, forward.

He quietly packed up his things, a faint smile on his face. There was much work to be done, but for the first time in a while, the future at work looked not just secure, but bright and exciting. Alex felt squarely in the center of that future, not watching helplessly from the sidelines but actively shaping it. And that realization was perhaps the greatest reward of all in this journey of adapting with AI.

Chapter 9: Imposter Syndrome

Alex shut down his laptop for the day, heart still thumping from the conversation that had just ended. He had just accepted the role as lead of the company's AI working group, an exciting opportunity, but now that the adrenaline was wearing off, a wave of imposter syndrome washed over him. The office was nearly empty this Friday evening. As he shrugged on his coat, he replayed the moment in his head: the company's VP had clapped him on the shoulder and said, "We need someone like you to guide us in using AI, Alex. You're the perfect fit."

Walking out to his car, Alex felt anything but a perfect fit. He fumbled with his keys, his palms sweaty. *Why me?* he thought. *I'm no AI expert.* His mind raced with doubts as he drove home. Sure, he had been an early champion of trying ChatGPT at work, but leading an AI initiative? That sounded like *a job for a tech guru, not someone who still thought GPT was the name of a file format* just a year ago.

By the time Alex stepped through his front door, his shoulders were tense. Maria was in the kitchen finishing up dinner preparations, and the house smelled of garlic and tomato sauce. Sophie was at the table doing homework. Maria looked up. "Hey hon, how was work?"

"It was... eventful," Alex replied, hanging up his coat. He kissed Maria's cheek and ruffled Sophie's hair on his way in.

"Dad's home!" Sophie grinned, but then she noticed his distracted expression. "Everything okay, Dad?"

"You look like you have a lot on your mind," Maria added, concern in her voice.

Alex sighed and joined them at the table. "Well, I have news," he said slowly. "They made me the lead of the new AI working group at the company."

Maria's face lit up. "Alex, that's wonderful! They clearly recognize your hard work."

Sophie jumped up and did a little cheer. "Go Dad! Mr. AI Lead!" She giggled, and Alex managed a weak chuckle.

"It *is* good news," he admitted. He poked absently at a piece of broccoli on Sophie's plate. "But honestly, I'm freaking out a little. I'm not sure I know what I'm doing. Everyone's going to expect me to be some AI expert overnight."

Maria placed a comforting hand on his arm. "You've learned a lot these past few months, right? Using ChatGPT for projects, reading those articles you told me about..."

"Yeah, but there's still so much I don't know," Alex said, staring down at the table. "What if they figure out I'm winging it?"

Sophie piped up softly, "Isn't that imposter syndrome, Dad? In my psychology class we learned it's when you feel not good enough even though you actually are."

Alex raised an eyebrow at her. Sometimes his 16-year-old's insight caught him by surprise. "Maybe it is," he conceded.

Over dinner, Maria and Sophie encouraged him with reminders of past successes and his ability to learn on the fly. Maria recalled how he once implemented a new project management system at work on short notice, he had figured it out and made it work. Sophie mentioned how she felt nervous being team leader for a school project but ended up doing a great job after she pushed through her self-doubt. Alex nodded at their stories, appreciating the support, but the gnawing worry remained.

Later that night, long after Sophie had gone to bed, Alex sat on the living room couch with his laptop. Maria was curled up reading beside him. Alex's mind was still churning. If he was going to lead an AI working group, he needed to seriously up his AI game, and fast.

Almost by instinct, he opened his browser and navigated to ChatGPT. The chat prompt blinked expectantly. Alex took a breath and typed: *"I just got put in charge of an AI initiative at work, but I'm not an expert. How can I quickly ramp up my AI knowledge and skills (without a technical background)?"*

He hit Enter and watched the familiar "thinking" dots. Within seconds, the AI replied with a list of suggestions:

1. Take an online AI fundamentals bootcamp designed for non-technical professionals.

2. Follow AI thought leaders and blogs to stay up-to-date on trends.

3. Practice using AI tools daily (e.g., try ChatGPT for small tasks) to build familiarity.

4. Join a community or find a mentor for sharing AI tips and guidance.

Alex zeroed in on the first suggestion: an online AI fundamentals course or bootcamp. A structured way to learn quickly sounded promising. He typed a follow-up: *"Any recommended AI bootcamps for someone like me?"*

ChatGPT responded promptly, mentioning a few programs by name. One stood out: a 6-week online AI bootcamp called "AI for Everyone Bootcamp," taught by an instructor named Blaze. The description said it was practical and non-technical, aimed at professionals who want to learn to use AI in their jobs without needing to code. Heart thumping with curiosity, Alex clicked the link.

The bootcamp's webpage was bold and modern. At the top, bold letters declared: "Level Up Your Career with AI, No Coding Required!" Alex scrolled, taking in the details. The program emphasized hands-on learning and promised to keep things jargon-free. A section listed the weekly sessions:

Bootcamp Curriculum (6 Weeks):

1. **AI Foundations & Ethics**: A plain-language guide to AI essentials, how to spot errors or bias, how to use AI responsibly, and understanding tools like ChatGPT.

2. **Writing with AI**: Using AI to draft emails, reports, summaries, and more, while preserving your voice.

3. **Visuals and Creativity**: Generate images, graphics, and layouts with simple tools. Create clean visuals for work or personal projects without needing design experience.

4. **Voice & Video:** Use AI to create narration, avatars, and short videos.

Improve communication with voiceovers or presentation-ready clips.

5. **Strategy & Growth:** Leverage AI for brainstorming, research, and practical problem-solving. Learn how to use AI as a thinking partner for work and life.

6. **Adaptive Action Plan:** Build your personal AI roadmap. Identify tasks AI can support, run small experiments, and create a plan to integrate AI into your daily work and routines.

Alex felt both excited and intimidated reading those session titles. They aligned perfectly with what he needed to learn, maybe even more. He continued scrolling and found testimonials from past participants under a "Success Stories" heading:

"I was a beginner with AI, but Blaze's bootcamp changed that." In six weeks, I went from feeling left behind to leading an AI project at my company. - Jasmine R., Marketing Manager

"I'm 58 and this bootcamp proved you can teach an 'old dog' new tricks. Blaze made complex concepts easy, and now I'm championing AI projects at work instead of fearing them." - Marco G., Operations Lead

Reading that someone in his late fifties had succeeded gave Alex hope; maybe this really was for anyone, not just the young tech crowd. The instructor, Blaze, was described as an AI consultant turned educator who was "passionate about demystifying AI for everyday professionals." A photo showed Blaze in his mid-30s, standing in front of a whiteboard with a big grin and animated hand gestures. The whole program exuded an upbeat, *you can do this* tone.

Maria glanced over at Alex's screen. "What's got you so hooked there?"

Alex rubbed his eyes and turned the laptop toward her. "This AI bootcamp. It's six weeks, online in the evenings. Taught by some guy named Blaze. It sounds… exactly like what I need, honestly."

Maria scanned the page. "Non-technical, practical, aimed at professionals… that does sound perfect for you."

"I'm seriously considering it," Alex said, then admitted, "but I'm also kind of scared. The topics look intense, and I'd probably be the oldest person in the class. What if it's full of young tech whizzes?"

Maria gave him a gentle but firm look. "Since when do you shy away from learning something new? You've always prided yourself on being adaptive, Alex. That's what your job needs now."

He managed a small smile. She wasn't wrong, his career had evolved many times, and he had always tried to adapt. But this felt different; diving into AI from scratch on a deadline felt like stepping into a foreign country without speaking the language. He felt like an imposter walking into a room full of experts, even if the bootcamp was meant for beginners.

Maria squeezed his hand. "Maybe you should talk to someone about it. What about Robert?"

Robert. Alex immediately thought of his long-time colleague and mentor. Robert was a senior manager who had seen countless technology waves come and go, and he had actually been the one to recommend Alex for this new role. If anyone would understand, it was him.

"You're right," Alex said. "Robert did tell me I could call him this weekend if I needed to talk."

Saturday morning, Alex did just that. He retreated to his small home office with a cup of coffee while Maria took Sophie to soccer practice. After staring at Robert's number for a minute, he pressed call.

"Alex! Perfect timing," Robert answered warmly. "I was just thinking about you. How are you feeling, lead man?"

Alex couldn't help but laugh a little. "Honestly, Robert, a little overwhelmed."

"I bet. New role, big expectations, it can stir up the old imposter syndrome," Robert said knowingly.

"Yeah, exactly," Alex sighed. "I keep thinking they should have picked someone more technical. I mean, I'm excited, but also terrified."

"I've been there," Robert said. "Let me tell you, *feeling* like an imposter just means you care about doing a good job. It doesn't mean you actually lack ability. Heck, I've been in tech for 30 years and I still felt out of my depth when we started talking AI strategy. But the truth is, you don't need to be a genius. You just need to be willing to learn and ask questions."

Alex felt a knot in his chest loosen slightly. Hearing Robert, someone he respected, admit to similar feelings was reassuring.

"I found this bootcamp, Robert," Alex said, and he described the AI for Everyone program. "Do you think it's a good idea for me to enroll?"

"I've heard of Blaze, actually," Robert said. "Some folks at a partner company took that bootcamp and loved it. I think investing in yourself is always a good idea. Six weeks isn't too long, and doing it in the evenings means it won't interfere with work much."

"I'm worried I'll struggle to keep up," Alex admitted quietly.

"You're worried you'll look foolish? That everyone will find out you're not an 'AI genius' overnight?" Robert chuckled. "Alex, feeling like an imposter means you care. But you've got to remember, they chose you for a reason. You're great at bringing people together and learning on the fly. Those skills matter here. And you'll *prove* any lingering fears wrong by doing the work. Keep willing to learn, and you'll prove those fears wrong."

Alex nodded along as Robert spoke, a sense of relief washing over him. He grabbed a pen and scribbled a quick line in his notes:

> Imposter syndrome is a sign I'm growing, not failing.

The act of writing it down made it feel more concrete.

Before hanging up, Robert added, "By the way, if you do join that bootcamp, maybe you can share a few insights with our working group each week. Teach us what you learn. It will help you solidify it and benefit everyone. Plus, it shows leadership you're proactively developing yourself."

A spark of motivation ignited in Alex. "You know, that's a great idea. I could do a short recap each Friday meeting."

Robert chuckled. "Look at you, already planning to teach others. You've got this, Alex."

After the call, Alex felt far more resolved. He sat at his laptop and clicked the "Enroll Now" button on the bootcamp site before he could second-guess himself. A registration form popped up. He filled in his details (Alex Harper, age 42, Project Manager) and when it asked for personal goals, he typed: *"I want to learn how to effectively use AI in my work and help my team adopt AI tools responsibly."* That sounded about right.

The price on the payment page made him gulp, it wasn't cheap, but he reminded himself it was an investment in his growth. The fact that the next cohort started Monday was perfect timing; so with a final confirmation click, it was done.

Almost immediately, an email arrived: "Welcome to AI for Everyone Bootcamp, Getting Started." The welcome email from Blaze was upbeat and encouraging, promising a fun, interactive learning journey and assuring him that no question was too basic. There were a few prep steps: join the cohort's Slack community, make sure Zoom was up to date, think about his goals for the course.

Alex joined the bootcamp's Slack community and skimmed introductions. Participants came from diverse fields, teachers, marketers, small business owners, not just techies, which was a relief. He posted a hello message, and almost immediately a finance professional replied, "Welcome, we got this!" Alex smiled at the quick camaraderie.

That night, as he got ready for bed, Alex pulled out his notebook. He wrote a few key thoughts to anchor himself for the week ahead:

> I don't need to be an expert overnight; I just need to be eager to learn.
>
> Stepping up to this challenge is how I grow, imposter syndrome and all.

"I enrolled in that bootcamp," he murmured in the darkness after he crawled into bed.

"That's great," Maria whispered, half-asleep, and gave his hand a squeeze. "I'm proud of you."

Alex lay there in the quiet, his mind calmer now. It was okay not to know everything yet, he was taking action to change that. The butterflies in his stomach were still there, but now they felt more like excitement than dread. Maybe, just maybe, he was ready for this challenge after all.

Chapter 10: AI Foundations & Ethics

Monday evening found Alex in his home office, nervously adjusting his webcam before clicking the Zoom link for the bootcamp's first session. The Zoom room flickered to life, and a gallery of friendly faces appeared. Some people looked as anxious as he felt; others waved or sipped coffee, gearing up for class after a workday.

"Welcome everyone!" boomed a voice as a lively figure with spiky black hair and an enormous smile appeared at the center of Alex's screen. This must be Blaze. He wore a bright orange t-shirt and radiated enough energy to light up the whole Zoom room.

"Good evening! I'm Blaze," he said, giving a little salute. "Congratulations on showing up for yourself. Over the next six weeks, we're going to demystify AI together." Blaze's enthusiasm was contagious; Alex felt himself sit up a bit straighter.

After brief introductions, Alex introduced himself quickly, and everyone was so friendly that he relaxed, the session kicked off. The title slide on Blaze's screen read:

AI Foundations & Ethics

"Alright," Blaze clapped once, "today we're going to get into AI foundation and how to use AI tools ethically. *Ethics* will actually be a recurring theme in our modules, as you will see."

"OK. Let's start with the basics. What even *is* AI, and how does it work? Don't worry, I'm not about to drop a ton of math on you. This is about understanding concepts in plain English."

Alex let out a breath he didn't realize he was holding. He had braced for an overly technical lecture, but Blaze kept it friendly and simple.

"Think of AI like the autocomplete on your phone, automatically completing individual words or entire sentences, but turbocharged," Blaze said. "AI does not think the way we do. It has read a huge amount of text from the internet, books, articles, and other publicly available material. When you type a prompt, it predicts the most likely response based on patterns it has seen. It does not truly understand meaning. It simply gets very good at guessing what should come next."

This clicked for Alex. He had used ChatGPT plenty of times, but thinking of it as a super advanced autocomplete made sense. Sometimes the responses really did sound like the model was following a script.

Blaze grinned and continued, "Now, because it's just predicting, sometimes it predicts wrong. Ever had your phone autocorrect to a completely weird word? AI models do that too, but in more elaborate ways. We have a term for it: hallucination." He wrote *Hallucination* on a virtual whiteboard. "In AI, a hallucination is when the system makes stuff up. It might give you an answer that sounds confident and plausible, but it's actually not true at all."

A few people chuckled or murmured in recognition. Blaze even shared an example of asking a chatbot for a book recommendation, and it confidently provided a completely fake title and author, a textbook AI hallucination. Alex felt a slight chill hearing that. He recalled times at work when he'd almost taken an AI output at face value. Understanding this now, he realized how important it was to double-check AI's answers.

Blaze moved to the next key topic: Bias. He grew a bit more serious. "AI models learn from human data. Unfortunately, human data contains flaws. Gender bias, racial bias, and cultural bias can sneak into outputs if the model learned from examples that included those biases. It is not intentional, but it still happens.If you see an output that seems biased or unfair, that's a red flag to adjust your approach or give feedback to the AI."

Alex thought of an example he'd heard about, an AI hiring tool that started favoring male applicants because it learned from biased past data. Blaze's warning hit home; Alex made a mental note to be vigilant about bias when his own team experimented with AI.

Then Blaze shifted to a topic Alex had not considered deeply: privacy and personal information.

"Let's take a moment to talk about how these tools handle your data," Blaze said. "There is a lot of confusion here, so let me clear this up simply."

Alex leaned forward.

"First, AI models do not build a personal profile of you," Blaze explained. "They do not remember who you are, where you live, or what you typed yesterday unless you explicitly enable features that save your history. However," he added, holding up a finger, "you can still accidentally overshare."

The chat lit up with nervous laughter.

"Think of it like this," Blaze continued. "Whatever you type into an AI tool should be something you would be comfortable emailing to a coworker. Do not paste in sensitive client information, social security numbers, medical details, passwords, or anything you would not hand to a stranger. AI tools are not trying to spy on you, but they cannot protect information that you voluntarily give them. That is one of the pitfalls."

Alex felt a jolt of recognition. He had seen coworkers paste client details into tools without a second thought.

"Another guideline is to anonymize information whenever you can," Blaze said. "Change names. Remove identifiers. Share only what the AI needs to help you. This keeps you safe and protects your clients."

Alex nodded slowly. He knew he had not always done this.

Next, Blaze wrote *Citations and Sources* on the board and asked, "How do you know if an AI's answer is trustworthy?" Someone answered that they'd fact-check or ask for sources.

"Exactly," Blaze said. He noted that some AI tools can provide sources, but even those should be double-checked. Sometimes an AI's cited source doesn't actually support its answer, another kind of hallucination. His rule of thumb: always verify important information independently. Never assume the AI is 100% correct just because it sounds confident.

Alex chuckled to himself; Blaze's description of an AI as a "smart person who has a tendency to bluff when they don't know something" was pretty on point.

Finally, Blaze typed the words "human-in-the-loop" on the whiteboard. "This means always keep a human involved, especially for important tasks. You don't turn AI loose without oversight," he explained.

"Think of it as a partnership: the AI can draft or suggest, but a human reviews and makes the final call. That way you catch mistakes or bias, and make sure everything fits the real-world context."

Alex was vigorously nodding. He remembered a recent near-mishap at work where an automated draft email almost went out with the wrong client name, a human caught it just in time. This concept of *human-in-the-loop* put a name to what he already suspected: AI is powerful, but it needs a human hand on the wheel.

Throughout the session, Blaze kept things engaging, asking questions and encouraging reactions in the chat. "Who here has tried ChatGPT or something similar at work?" he asked at one point. A bunch of virtual hands went up, including Alex's. One student admitted she had fed an AI tool her entire medical history without thinking. Blaze reassured her that mistakes happen when people do not fully understand how the tools work.

By the end of the session, Alex felt grounded. Not an expert, but no longer in the dark. His notebook now held a clear set of foundations.

AI predicts text; it does not understand it

Hallucinations are normal and must be checked

AI can reflect human bias

Important facts must be verified

Personal information should be protected

A human must always review the AI's output

He finally felt like he had a firm starting point and safe guardrails for what would come next.

At home later that night, after class, Alex made a cup of tea in the kitchen. Sophie was there finishing a bowl of ice cream.

"You were on a call for a while," Sophie said. "Was that your AI class?"

"Yep, first session," Alex smiled, dunking his tea bag. "We talked about how tools like ChatGPT actually work."

"Really? How do they work?" Sophie closed her textbook, clearly more interested in her dad's new class than her homework.

Alex explained in the same terms Blaze had used. "It's kind of like the autocomplete on your phone, but much more advanced. The AI has read a ton of stuff from the internet, and when you ask it something, it's trying to predict a good answer based on all that training. But it doesn't actually *know* if something is true, it's just guessing what sounds right."

"Like a parrot that doesn't understand the words but can say them," Sophie offered.

"Exactly," Alex chuckled. "A very clever parrot."

Sophie frowned thoughtfully. "So is that why Mr. Diaz, my English teacher, said we can't just use ChatGPT to write our essays? Because it might be wrong or just… not really our own thinking?"

"Precisely," Alex said. "If you just copied what it wrote, aside from being cheating, you could be copying mistakes or made-up stuff. Plus, your teacher wants *your* brain to do the work, not a tool."

Sophie nodded. "A friend tried using ChatGPT for a history paper and it gave her all the dates wrong until I insisted she double-check them, saving her grade."

Alex raised his eyebrows. "Good catch. That's exactly what we discussed: the AI can hallucinate or mess up facts, so you have to verify."

"Well, I'd never just trust it to do my work," Sophie said. "Maybe to get ideas or check grammar, but not to just hand in."

Alex smiled. It was rewarding to see Sophie instinctively understand the ethics. "That's the right approach. Use it to help with ideas or fix sentences, but focus on learning, and use the AI to support your work, not do it for you."

Sophie yawned. "Got it, Dad. Still, it's kind of cool you're learning this stuff. Maybe you can help me on the next project, within the rules, of course."

"Deal," Alex laughed. "Night, Soph."

"Night, Dad." Sophie headed off to bed, pausing to add with a smirk, "Don't stay up too late nerding out with your AI friend."

On Friday afternoon, Alex convened the weekly AI working group meeting at the office. It was his first meeting leading as the new head of the group, but thanks to the bootcamp session, he came armed with something to share. All five other team members were present: Jason and Linda who had volunteered from the beginning, Raj from IT, junior accountant Priya, and Robert, who had tentatively offered his support, but was unsure how he could contribute. Robert gave Alex an encouraging nod as the meeting began.

Alex cleared his throat. "I thought I'd start by sharing a few insights I picked up this week from an AI fundamentals course I'm taking. Just some basics that might help us all get on the same page."

He saw a few surprised but curious looks, apparently not everyone knew he'd enrolled in a course, but the reaction seemed positive.

"I'll keep it simple," Alex said. He proceeded to explain in everyday language what he had learned about how AI like ChatGPT works, much as Blaze had done. He even borrowed Blaze's analogy: describing it as a supercharged autocomplete that's read the whole internet.

He saw nods around the table. Raj from IT nodded and mentioned that tech folks call those confident mistakes "hallucinations", confirming Alex's point. Alex reiterated that this is why they must always double-check important information from AI outputs.

Linda shared that she'd used an AI for a corporate audit report and it suggested some outdated tax practices she had to fix. It was a relief to her to realize the bias was in the tool, not just her imagination. Alex agreed, noting that being aware of these limitations actually empowers them to use AI wisely instead of blindly trusting it.

Alex also emphasized the human-in-the-loop idea: "So, if we use an AI tool to draft something, we all understand someone has to review it before it goes out, right? It might save us time on a first draft, but we own the final product."

By the end of his mini-presentation, Alex noticed everyone was paying attention and even jotting notes. The imposter syndrome that had nagged him a week ago was notably quieter now. He *did* know this stuff, and he was able to convey it usefully to others.

"So those are a few foundations of AI I wanted to share," Alex concluded. "If we keep these in mind, we'll avoid a lot of pitfalls as we start using these tools in our workflows."

There were murmurs of agreement around the table. He could see Linda already sharing an example of an AI tool she wanted to try (with proper oversight), and Raj was asking how they might verify outputs efficiently. Alex chimed in here and there, guiding the discussion with his newly acquired knowledge.

As the meeting continued, Alex applied his new knowledge, suggesting a human should monitor an internal AI chatbot's answers, and proposing a review process to check any AI-generated marketing copy. The team seemed to appreciate these concrete ideas.

After the meeting, Alex felt a mix of relief and pride. He had contributed real value today. By learning and sharing his knowledge, he was helping his whole team adapt to AI more responsibly.

Walking back to his desk, Robert fell into step beside him. "You've got a knack for explaining this, Alex," he said quietly. "Keep it up."

Alex smiled. Coming from Robert, that meant a lot. "Thanks. It feels good to not just be winging it, I actually have some foundation now."

All in all, it had been a whirlwind week: he had gone from doubting himself to actively leading conversations about AI at work. And it was only the first class of the bootcamp. As he packed up to head home, Alex felt a sense of momentum. He couldn't wait to see what the next session would bring.

That evening, he wrote a couple of lines in his notebook to capture the week's lessons:

> AI is a powerful tool, but it needs human judgment at every step.
>
> Learn the limits of the tool, and you'll know how best to use it.

He smiled; those lines summed up exactly what he'd learned. With that, he closed his notebook. One successful week down, and he was already looking forward to the next session.

Chapter 11: Writing with AI

Monday evening Alex was back at his computer for the second bootcamp session. He felt a lot less nervous this time, recognizing Blaze, of course, Mia, Tasha, and Jordan, as he logged in. The Zoom room filled with these now-familiar faces and Blaze's energetic presence front-and-center. Tonight's title slide read:

`Writing with AI, Level Up Communication`

Blaze kicked off the session with his trademark enthusiasm. "Good to see you all again! How did the homework go? Anyone apply AI in their work this week?"

A few people unmuted to share short updates: Mia mentioned she used ChatGPT to brainstorm ideas for a project proposal, and Tasha (the finance professional who had welcomed Alex in Slack) said she tried it to draft a tricky client email. Alex shared that he'd used an AI tool to summarize a lengthy report for his team, it saved him a lot of time, and after he polished the summary, his colleagues found it really helpful.

"Fantastic," Blaze said, nodding. "Small wins like that build up. Now, let's dive into tonight's topic: using AI to *write*."

Alex straightened in his chair. This session was what he'd been looking forward to, practical guidance on writing tasks, which made up a big chunk of his workday.

Blaze began with a question: "How many of you have stared at a blank screen not sure how to start an email or report?" Nearly every hand (virtual or otherwise) went up, prompting chuckles. "Me too," Blaze laughed. "Writer's block, tedious report writing, updating your resume, all that can be made easier with AI. But, and it's a big *but*, you have to guide the AI. AI doesn't think for you, it helps express your thinking."

He emphasized that phrase on his slide: "express your thinking." Alex dutifully put a star next to that quote in his notes.

Blaze then launched into examples. The first scenario was "*Email Makeover.*" He showed a sample: a clunky, overly formal draft email to a client that rambled. "If I got this email, I'd probably skim it and miss the point," Blaze said, smiling. "Let's fix it."

He copied the draft into a ChatGPT window on screen and added a prompt: "Make this email more concise and friendly in tone, while keeping all the key points." In a blink, the AI produced a revised email: it was half the length, clearly worded, and had a warm but professional tone.

There were impressed murmurs in the chat. "See that?" Blaze pointed out. "The AI didn't invent new ideas, it just helped say what I wanted to say, but better. You *could* do that on your own, but it might take you a few edits and a lot of time. AI gives you that polished draft quickly."

Alex found himself grinning. He'd used ChatGPT for email drafts before, but seeing the transformation side-by-side was affirming. He made a note of the prompt Blaze used for later.

Next up: summarizing and outlining. Blaze described how you can feed AI a long article or report and ask for a summary or key bullet points. "Just remember, you're the expert on what's important," he cautioned. "So review the summary and make sure it didn't miss anything critical to your needs."

Jordan asked via chat, *"Can I ask it to write a whole report if I give it a topic?"* Blaze shook his head gently. "You can ask, but you probably won't get something truly useful without your input. It'll be generic because the AI doesn't have the specifics of your situation. And more importantly, that would be the AI doing the thinking, not you. The goal is to let AI assist, not replace, your judgment." He reiterated Blaze's golden rule: *YOU* remain the driver; AI is just the helper. A few people reacted with thumbs-up emojis in agreement.

Another scenario on Blaze's slide: *"Resume and Cover Letter Helper."* Blaze chuckled, "How many of you have helped a friend with their resume or struggled with your own?" Alex immediately thought of Mark. He raised his hand as did many others.

Blaze gave tips on using AI for resumes in a smart way. "Don't just say 'write me a resume' and expect magic. Instead, use AI to improve specific parts. For example, if your resume says, 'Managed a team,' you might prompt: *'Rewrite this bullet to highlight a result: managed a team of 5 to deliver Project X 2 weeks early.'* The AI could turn that into something like, 'Led a team of 5 to deliver Project X two weeks ahead of schedule, improving time-to-market.' Now it's quantified and sounds impact-driven. But notice, *you* provided the key facts (the team size, the early delivery). The AI just helped frame it better."

Alex nearly applauded at that example. He couldn't wait to try a similar approach with Mark's resume.

Blaze even had the class practice in pairs. In a short breakout, Alex and Tasha used AI to draft a thank-you email to a colleague and saw how quickly a polished note came together when they guided the tool with the right points.

By the end of class, Alex felt energized. Writing had always been something he could do, but having AI as a sort of on-call editor or wordsmith could save so much time. He just had to remember Blaze's golden rule: he was still the author; the AI was the assistant.

For homework, Blaze asked everyone to pick a piece of writing they needed to do in the coming week, anything from an email to a report, and use AI to help with one aspect of it. "Then next time, we'll share what worked and what didn't," he said. "And remember, you're still the one doing the thinking. AI is your tool, not your replacement."

After class, Alex barely had time to digest everything Blaze had covered before he turned his attention to Mark. He shot him a text: *"Hey, learned some new AI tricks for resumes tonight. Want to refine yours?"* Mark's reply came almost instantly: *"Yes please!"*

An hour later, Mark was at Alex's dining table with his laptop and a printout of his updated resume, the one they had polished weeks ago. It was already much stronger than before, but now Alex saw opportunities he hadn't recognized then.

Mark eased into the chair. "I feel like it's close… but I'm still not getting many callbacks."

Alex nodded. "Totally normal. Most companies use applicant tracking systems now, so a good resume still needs tuning for each job posting."

Mark groaned. "Don't tell me I have to rewrite the whole thing for every application."

"Not rewrite," Alex said, smiling. "*Retarget.* And AI can handle most of the heavy lifting."

He pulled up ChatGPT in his left window with his browser window showing on the right. "Watch this. This is one of the advanced techniques Blaze showed us today."

He uploaded Mark's resume into ChatGPT and pasted in the job description for a logistics supervisor role for which Mark was applying. Finally, he typed:

"Compare this resume to the job posting. Identify missing keywords and suggest targeted improvements to align the resume with the role."

ChatGPT responded with a clear list of skill gaps and keyword suggestions:

- Missing terms: *logistics optimization, cross-department coordination, KPI tracking, workflow automation.*
- Suggested additions to bullets.
- Specific ways to tailor achievements to match the job posting.

Mark leaned in. "It can do that?"

Alex smirked. "It just did."

He picked one suggestion, adding KPI tracking to the processing-time bullet, and prompted:

"Rewrite this bullet to incorporate KPI tracking while keeping it truthful:

'Led a team of 5 in warehouse operations, improving order processing time by 15%.' "

ChatGPT returned: *"Led a team of 5 in warehouse operations, improving order processing time by 15% and introducing KPI tracking methods to monitor workflow efficiency."*

Mark's eyes widened. "Okay… that's actually really good."

"It's still your work," Alex said. "Just framed the way the job wants to read it."

Next, Alex showed him something new: a positioning statement, a short piece Blaze had said many applicants overlook.

"It's like a headline at the top of your resume. Helps hiring managers understand who you are in one line."

He prompted: "Create a professional positioning statement for a logistics operations supervisor with experience in process improvement, warehouse leadership, and cross-functional coordination."

ChatGPT generated: *"Logistics operations leader specializing in process optimization, team development, and cross-functional coordination to drive consistent, measurable performance improvements."*

Mark read it twice. "Can I steal that?"

"It's yours," Alex said, laughing.

They added it to the top of the resume and made a few minor tweaks to keep it in Mark's voice.

Finally, Alex demonstrated how to generate role-specific bullets using the job description itself:

"Rewrite this bullet using terminology from the job posting while keeping content factual:

'Oversaw inventory management and optimized stock levels, reducing excess inventory by 10%.' "

ChatGPT rewrote it as: *"Oversaw inventory management and aligned stock levels with operational demand forecasts, reducing excess inventory by 10% and supporting improved fulfillment accuracy."*

"That sounds like something they'd want to hear," Mark said. "That's the point," Alex said. "We're not making anything up, we're translating your work into their language."

They didn't overhaul the whole resume, just sharpened it with these advanced techniques. After twenty minutes, the difference was obvious. The resume read cleaner, tighter, and, thanks to the keyword alignment, much more relevant.

Mark exhaled, a mix of relief and renewed confidence. "I feel like I finally have a fighting chance."

"You do," Alex said. "And next time you see a job posting, don't rewrite everything, just give the AI the job description and ask what to adjust. Two minutes, max."

Mark grinned. "I owe you a beer if this gets me interviews."

"Make it two," Alex said, closing his laptop. "One for me, one for Blaze."

The next day, Saturday, Alex was typing up a few class notes in the living room when Maria came in from her workshop carrying a notebook and her phone. She had that thoughtful look Alex knew well.

"Hey," Maria said, "can I steal you for a few minutes? I want your AI advice on something for the candle business."

"Sure!" Alex closed his laptop. He loved that Maria was now curious about these tools too. "What's up?"

"Well," Maria sat down, tucking a stray lock of hair behind her ear, "I need to write a description for my new holiday candle for the website, and maybe an email blurb. You know writing those little marketing snippets is my least favorite part of running this business."

Alex did know, Maria often agonized over getting the wording just right. "We can absolutely use AI for that," he said excitedly. "Tell me about the candle."

Maria showed him a photo on her phone of a lovely mason-jar candle with a sprig of cinnamon stick tied to it. "It's called 'Winter Warmth.' It's cinnamon vanilla scented. Hand-poured soy wax, of course. And it has a wood wick that crackles like a tiny fireplace. I want the description to feel cozy and festive."

Alex opened ChatGPT. "Alright, let's feed it the basics." He typed: *"Write a short, cozy product description for a hand-poured soy candle called Winter Warmth. Highlight the cinnamon vanilla scent and crackling wood wick, and convey a warm, holiday feeling."*

They watched as the AI composed a paragraph:

"Experience the cozy embrace of Winter Warmth. Hand-poured with all-natural soy wax, this candle fills your home with the comforting aroma of cinnamon and vanilla, just like holiday baking. Its wooden wick adds a gentle crackle, evoking the warmth of a fireplace on a winter's night. Light Winter Warmth to envelop your space in a soothing glow and festive scent, the perfect touch of holiday cheer for those cold nights."

Maria's eyes widened as Alex read the description out loud. "That's… actually really good," she said. "It hit all the points: cozy, cinnamon and vanilla, the crackling wick, holidays."

"And it took, what, ten seconds to write?" Alex grinned.

"I'll tweak a word or two so it sounds like *me*, but honestly I might not need to change much," Maria said, clearly impressed. "This just solved in seconds what would've taken me an hour and three mugs of coffee to write."

Alex chuckled. "Now you see why I'm so keen on this AI stuff."

Maria gave him an impulsive hug. "My techie husband to the rescue. Thank you."

"Anytime," Alex said, hugging her back. "We can try it for your marketing email too. Maybe something like: 'Announcing our Winter Warmth candle…'"

"Oh, yes please," Maria said. "I'm officially converted. Maybe I should join an AI bootcamp too!" she added jokingly.

"You'd be great at it," Alex winked.

That coming Monday, Alex decided to take another proactive step at work. Over the weekend he had created a one-page document titled "AI Writing Assistant, Prompt Tips" for his team, summarizing some of the writing-related AI tricks he'd learned. It included a few example prompts and best practices:

- *Email Draft:* "Help me draft a polite email to thank a client for their feedback on our product, and address their concern about delivery delays."

- *Report Summary:* "Summarize the key points of the attached report in 5 bullet points, focusing on marketing insights."

- *Resume Bullet Improvement:* "Rewrite the following resume bullet to be achievement-focused: Managed a team of 5 in retail sales (add any measurable results)."

At the top, he highlighted Blaze's cardinal rule: "AI is a tool to express your ideas, you provide the thinking, it provides the wording."

He emailed this cheat sheet to the AI working group and a few other colleagues who had shown interest in his tips.

The response was immediate and enthusiastic. His colleagues loved the guide. Nina from customer service told Alex it was "gold" after it helped her craft a tricky customer email, and even Robert mentioned that one of Alex's tips saved him a couple of hours on a report. Alex's cheeks warmed at the praise, and he felt a surge of pride.

Just a couple of weeks ago, he had felt completely behind on all this. Now he was empowering others with what he'd learned.

As Alex wrapped up work that day, he reflected on how far he'd come in such a short time. Two bootcamp sessions down, and he was already applying the knowledge at work, at home, and helping a friend. He was starting to truly feel like an "adaptive professional."

That evening, Alex opened his notebook and jotted down a few new insights, in bold for emphasis:

AI can help me write and refine, but *my* ideas and intentions lead the way.

Use AI to amplify my voice, not replace it.

He capped his pen and smiled at the words. They summed up exactly what he'd learned in this chapter of his journey. With AI as an assistant, he was communicating more effectively than ever, but it was still *him* doing the thinking and guiding the outcome. Each experiment and each shared tip made him more confident that he could navigate this AI-powered world responsibly and well.

He closed the notebook, feeling that forward momentum again. Two sessions down, and he couldn't wait to see what the rest of the bootcamp, and his own AI initiatives at work, would bring next.

Chapter 12: Visuals & Creativity

Alex logged in early for the next AI bootcamp session, feeling eager and a bit jittery. On the projector screen, a series of eye-catching images cycled: a futuristic cityscape, a cat in a suit giving a presentation, an abstract company logo with vibrant colors. Each image looked expertly crafted. Blaze took his place at the front and gestured to the montage with a grin.

"Pretty cool, right?" Blaze said, pausing on the image of the cat in a suit. "None of these visuals were made by a human. They're all generated by AI."

A ripple of murmurs passed through the class. Alex leaned forward, intrigued. Blaze clicked his title slide and the cat picture shrank to the corner.

AI for Visuals & Creativity

"Welcome to the world of AI-generated visuals," Blaze began. "Today's session is about creating images and designs with AI. You don't have to be a graphic designer to make something that looks great." He looked around the room. "Everyone is now a visual communicator in some way. In fact, even people in non-design roles are often expected to have *some* design ability. That can be lot of pressure if you've never created a visual or simple design before! Thankfully, AI can help."

Alex nodded, remembering how often he needed a graphic for a presentation at work and ended up using dull stock images. The idea that he could make custom visuals himself was exciting.

Blaze flipped to the next slide, which showed names of popular text-to-image tools: Midjourney, DALL·E, Stable

Diffusion, and a logo for Canva. "First, let's talk text-to-image generation. These tools take a description you write, the *prompt*, and output an image. For example, if I type 'a purple dragon reading a book in a library, cartoon style', the AI will draw it." The projector displayed exactly that: a whimsical illustration of a purple dragon engrossed in a book amidst library shelves. A few people chuckled in surprise.

"Under the hood, these generators learned from millions of images, but we won't get technical," Blaze said. "The key is what we *can do* with them." He clicked to a list titled "Practical Uses" and highlighted each point:

- Mockups & prototypes: "Need a concept illustration of a product or a quick sketch of an idea? Describe it, and AI drafts an image. Great for visualizing ideas early."
- Presentations & reports: "Instead of spending hours hunting for the perfect stock photo, you can generate a custom illustration in minutes."
- Social media content: "Want an eye-catching graphic for a blog or Instagram? AI image generators can produce unique visuals on the fly. It eliminates the hassle of finding stock photos for every post."

Alex scribbled in his notebook:

> AI can draft images fast, no design degree needed.

Blaze smiled at the note-taking. "Now, AI won't replace professional designers, entirely! But it will handle a lot of grunt work and enable the rest of us to do more on our own." He added, "One marketing expert noted that it's so much easier now to sketch a concept with AI and show it to your boss for feedback, versus creating multiple polished drafts from scratch. You can iterate quickly on ideas."

Alex could relate to that. He recalled times he spent days refining slides or graphics. With AI, he could get a rough idea out in minutes and refine from there.

Blaze then pointed to the last item on the slide: Canva. "Who here has used Canva?" A few hands, including Alex's, went up. "Great. Canva isn't a text-to-image generator like Midjourney, but it's a popular design platform that has embraced AI. Their mission is to empower non-designers to create great visuals. They provide templates for everything, presentations, flyers, social media posts, and recently added AI features like a Magic Design tool and even a text-to-image option."

He explained how businesses use it: "At FedEx, they rolled out Canva company-wide and drastically cut down the backlog of design requests. The Canva website proclaims that FedEx was able to reduce internal design requests by 77% because people could now create their own visual content themselves using Canva. The creative team was freed up to focus on big projects instead of tiny graphics. The takeaway: tools like Canva let you create content in minutes instead of waiting days."

Blaze transitioned to a demo. He opened a text-to-image tool on the big screen. "Let's generate something together. Say Alex here needs an image for an AI presentation at work." Alex felt a jolt as Blaze mentioned him. "What kind of visual would help get your point across?"

Alex thought, then said, "Maybe a friendly robot working with a person, to show AI-human collaboration. Something clean and modern."

"Great idea," Blaze replied. On screen he typed: "Professional illustration of a friendly robot assisting a businessperson at a computer, modern flat art style." After a few seconds, four variations appeared. The class murmured in approval. Each image showed a friendly-looking robot alongside an office worker in front of a computer. In one, the robot pointed at a chart on a screen while the person nodded; in another, the robot handed the person a coffee. The designs were on-brand and engaging.

Alex was amazed. "That first one is nearly perfect for my slide," he said, eyes wide. It looked like something a graphic artist might have spent hours on.

"And we got it in under a minute," Blaze noted. "Now, sometimes the first try isn't exactly right. If needed, you can tweak your prompt or try different styles and generate again. Prompt crafting is a bit of an art, but you get better with practice."

He clicked on the selected image to enlarge it. "Notice anything odd here before you use it?" The class leaned in. One student pointed out the robot's hand holding the coffee looked a little distorted. Blaze nodded, "Good eye. AI images can have weird artifacts, messed-up hands, gibberish text if you asked for words, that sort of thing. Always review and, if it's something important, consider touching it up or generating a new one. Don't blindly trust every pixel."

Alex jotted another note: Review AI visuals closely for strange details.

Next, Blaze brought up a slide with a crucial topic: ethical considerations with graphics. "Just because we can generate images easily doesn't mean we can forget responsibility," he said. The slide had a short list, and Blaze elaborated on each:

- Be transparent: "Don't pass off AI art as hand-made when it's not. If you use an AI-generated image in client work or public materials, it's best to disclose that. In some places, laws are coming that require AI-generated content to be labeled."

- Don't deceive: "Avoid using AI to create fake realities. You all heard about that viral image of Pope Francis in a designer puffer jacket? That picture was generated with Midjourney and fooled a lot of people. It was harmless in that case, but it showed how easily images can spread misinformation, and why we need to handle these tools with care and integrity."."

- Use as a tool, not a weapon: "Don't use AI images to defame or impersonate people. We have a responsibility to uphold trust. These tools should augment our creativity, not undermine truth."

Alex was struck by the Pope example. He remembered Mark sending him a link to that image, and how real it looked until you noticed the tiny flaws. Hearing Blaze bring it up reminded Alex of the ethics discussion from the first session. He realized that part of adapting to AI meant slowing down and using good judgment, both when viewing content and when creating it. Not everything that looks real is actually real, and Blaze's reminder about staying honest and responsible with these tools stayed with him. It made Alex confident that he could champion AI at work while still honoring the ethical boundaries he now understood more clearly.

After a few final questions from the class, Blaze wrapped up. "Tonight, experiment with an image generator or try out a design on Canva," he encouraged. "You won't break anything. Worst case, you get some funky pictures; best case, you make something useful or inspiring. The only way to get comfortable is to play around. Have fun with it."

As Alex packed up his laptop, Blaze gave him a fist bump. "Let me know how that slide turns out," Blaze said warmly.

"Will do," Alex replied with a grin, feeling enthusiastic about putting this into practice.

That evening at home, Alex proudly showed Maria the AI-generated illustration he planned to use. It was the image of the robot assisting the office worker.

"You made that?" Maria asked, raising her eyebrows.

"The AI made it, I just wrote a prompt," Alex said, giving credit where it was due.

"Well, it looks totally professional," she remarked, clearly impressed. "Your team is going to love it."

At the dining table, Sophie was working on a school project surrounded by markers and a poster board. "Whatcha got there?" Alex asked her.

"It's for a science project on saving the bees," Sophie sighed. She had drawn a big title *'Bee the Change!"* but was struggling with the artwork. "I wanted to draw a cute bee cartoon, but I'm not great at drawing."

Alex and Maria exchanged a glance. "Maybe AI can help you too," Alex said. He sat beside Sophie with his laptop. "There are image generators for art. Want to try making a bee picture with me?"

Sophie's face lit up. "Really? That'd be awesome!"

Alex opened a kid-friendly online image generator. "Okay, describe what you want."

Sophie thought for a moment, then typed: "Cute cartoon honey bee on a flower with Earth in the background." They clicked Generate. In seconds, several bright illustrations appeared: cheerful bees with globes and flowers, just as she imagined.

"These are so cool!" Sophie squealed. She picked her favorite, a smiling bee perched on a sunflower, with a small Earth icon behind it, and Alex printed it out to fit on her poster.

As Sophie carefully cut out the image, Maria looked on with a mix of amazement and caution. "Is it alright for her to use an AI-generated picture for school? I mean, is that allowed?" she asked Alex quietly.

He considered it. "It's original in that she didn't copy someone else's work; an AI created it based on her idea. But it's good to be transparent." Alex turned to Sophie. "In a corner of your poster, just write that the bee image was made with an AI tool. That way you're being honest about where it came from."

"Okay, I can do that," Sophie nodded. "My teacher said we should note our sources for images, so I'll just say 'Bee image created with AI'."

Maria smiled. "Sounds good. It's like citing a source, except the source is a computer program."

A short while later, Sophie's poster was complete with the vibrant AI-assisted artwork. "Thank you, this is so much better than my drawing," she said, giving her dad a quick hug before trotting off to pack her school bag.

With Sophie's crisis averted, Alex joined Maria on the couch. She had her laptop open to Canva. "So, I was thinking of making a label for my candle business," Maria said. She had been selling homemade scented candles as a side project, and she wanted a simple logo or label design. "I signed up for Canva like you suggested a while back, but I haven't really used it. Think we could give it a try now?"

"Absolutely," Alex said, glad to help. They created a new design on Canva's interface, choosing a small product label template. It had a pretty layout with space for text and a little graphic. Maria replaced the placeholder text with "Maria's Aromatherapy Candles" in an elegant font.

"For the graphic, let's use something related to lavender since that's your signature scent," Alex suggested. He showed her Canva's built-in Text to Image feature. They typed "simple icon of a lit candle with lavender flowers, flat design" and hit Generate. Within moments, Canva provided a neat little illustration: a purple candle surrounded by sprigs of lavender. It fit perfectly with the label's style.

Maria dragged the new icon into place and adjusted the colors to match her theme. In less than 20 minutes, she had a finished label design ready to print. It looked artisanal and professional at the same time.

"I can't believe I just designed my own label!" Maria exclaimed, both thrilled and a bit stunned. She admired the result on the screen. "And it actually looks good."

"It looks great," Alex assured her. "And you did it without having to hire a designer or spend weeks learning Photoshop."

Maria chuckled. "I'll admit, I felt a bit like I was cheating not doing it from scratch. But for a small project like this, it makes so much sense. If I ever turn it into a big business, I can work with a professional designer. But at least now I have a solid idea to start with."

"Exactly," said Alex. "These tools give you a head start. You can always bring in an expert later if you need, but you've just saved yourself a ton of time and money by doing the first draft yourself."

As the night grew late, Alex reflected on how much had changed in one day. At work he'd be able to create a slide visual on his own; at home his daughter made a better school project, and his wife jumped into graphic design, all with AI's help.

Before turning in, Alex opened his notebook to jot a final takeaway from the day:

> AI image tools = creativity boost and time saver, just use them ethically.

He closed the notebook with a contented smile. Adapting to these new tools felt empowering. As he headed to bed, he was already looking forward to the next bootcamp session on voice and video, wondering what new possibilities it would bring.

Chapter 13: Voice and Video

"Good afternoon, everyone," Blaze boomed, but something was off, his lips hadn't moved. Alex blinked in surprise, then realized the voice greeting the class wasn't coming from Blaze himself, but from a speaker. On the projector screen, a video had started playing: a friendly-looking avatar of a woman in a business suit stood against a plain background, speaking in a clear voice.

"Welcome to our session on AI for voice and avatars," the on-screen woman said. Her lip sync was nearly perfect. If Alex didn't know better, he might have assumed it was a real person doing a video call. The avatar smiled and continued, "I'm Ava, an AI-generated presenter. Blaze invited me to help demonstrate today's topic."

The real Blaze, standing off to the side, crossed his arms with a satisfied grin as the class watched, fascinated. After a minute, he paused the video. "So, what do you think? Pretty realistic, huh?"

A few people murmured appreciatively. One classmate said, "I honestly thought it was a real person for the first few seconds."

Blaze stepped back to center stage. "That, my friends, was entirely AI-generated. The voice, the face, the movements, all of it. I typed a script, chose an avatar style, and it created that video automatically." He pointed at the frozen image of Ava on the screen. "This is what today is about: text-to-speech and AI avatars. Essentially, getting AI to speak for you, in audio or on video."

Alex felt a tingle of excitement. He had read about AI voices and deepfakes, but seeing a custom avatar in action was something else. It was like a glimpse of the future of presentations and training content.

Blaze launched into the lesson. He explained that text-to-speech (TTS) technology has evolved rapidly. "We've had robotic GPS voices and virtual assistants for years. But now, AI can produce speech that's extremely human-like, with emotion, intonation, even breaths. It can also generate a visual avatar that looks like a real person or a cartoon, and have it speak the words."

AI Voice & Video

He clicked to his title slide that listed examples: well-known TTS services and platforms like ElevenLabs, Amazon Polly, Google Wavenet, and avatar video generators like Synthesia and D-ID. "These names aren't as important as what they let you do," Blaze said, "which is turn written text into spoken presentations or narrations, without needing a camera or a microphone."

He enumerated some professional uses:

- Voiceovers for videos: "AI voices are used to narrate explainers, ads, or training videos. Instead of hiring a voice actor for every minor update, you can generate a high-quality narration on your laptop."
- Virtual presenters: "As you saw with Ava, you can create a talking head video without being on camera. This is great for things like e-learning modules or product demos. It's you *presenting*, but not actually you. You could even

pick an avatar that looks like a friendly teacher or a cartoon character for different audiences."

- Multilingual content: "One powerful aspect, you can instantly have the AI speak in other languages. Type your script, then have the avatar or voice 'speak' it in Spanish, Chinese, French, you name it, with accurate accents. This means you can create training or marketing content for global teams without needing a translator voiceover. AI video platforms make it easy to generate the same video in many languages."

Alex scribbled in his notebook:

AI voices = quick narration in any language.

Blaze continued, "Think about the efficiency. Creating a professional video used to require a whole production team. Now, anyone can do it with these tools." He flashed another slide showing a cost comparison: Traditional Video vs. AI Video. "One vendor claims AI video production is 50–80% cheaper than doing it the old way. A five-minute training video that might cost $5,000 to film could be made for a fraction of that with AI. And in hours, not weeks."

Some class members exchanged astonished looks. Blaze chuckled, "I know, it sounds like a dream for budget-strapped teams. And it is, but there are caveats we'll discuss. Still, the time and cost savings are very real."

He then addressed the elephant in the room: quality. "So, does this replace real human presenters completely? Not exactly. The tech is good, but not perfect. Avatars can seem a little stiff or uncanny at times, meaning something about them feels a bit off to viewers." He unpaused the video of Ava and let it play silently while pointing out features. "Notice her eyes blink at regular intervals and she gestures, but there's a subtle lack of true spontaneity. Some people pick up on that and find it creepy. How many of you felt a tiny bit uncomfortable, even if you were impressed?"

Alex raised his hand along with Jordan and Mia. It was true; as impressive as Ava was, there was a certain lifelessness in the eyes that gave him a moment's pause.

"Right. That's the uncanny valley effect. The avatar is almost human, but not quite, and our brains sense it," Blaze explained. "Now, purely audio voices don't have that visual problem, but they have their own tell-tales, maybe they sometimes put emphasis on the wrong word or sound too consistently even-toned. So, while AI voices are amazingly lifelike, they're not 100% fooling everyone yet."

Blaze advanced to a slide titled "ethical considerations with voice and video". "As with everything, we have to use these tools wisely." He highlighted a few points:

- Disclosure and transparency: "If you're using an AI voice or avatar in client-facing content, be upfront about it. It's about trust. In some sectors, like political ads, there are already laws that AI-generated video or audio must come with a disclaimer. And broader laws are being proposed to forbid making AI replicas of real people without consent, for instance, cloning a CEO's voice to make a fake announcement is a big no-no."

- Consent for voice cloning: "Speaking of which, never clone someone's voice without their permission. It's technically possible to sample a few minutes of someone talking and create a voice that sounds just like them. But doing that behind their back is unethical and could be illegal. Only use voice cloning on your own voice or with full permission."

- Avoid deception and harm: "We've all heard of deepfake videos or audio used maliciously, like scam calls where criminals mimic a loved one's voice. The FBI has warned that AI is making these scams more believable. So, we as ethical professionals should never contribute to that dark side. Use AI voice tech to uplift and inform, not to trick."

Alex absorbed Blaze's words, thinking of the news article Mark had shared about scammers cloning voices. It was reassuring that Blaze emphasized these points. The power of this technology was incredible, but so was the potential for abuse.

To lighten the mood, Blaze grinned and added, "Also, don't use an AI avatar to pretend you're attending two meetings at once. Tempting as it may be!" The class laughed, picturing an avatar of themselves nodding along in a Zoom meeting while they snuck off to do other things. Blaze wagged a finger humorously, "It might fool some people, but if you get caught, well... career suicide."

He concluded the session by inviting everyone to experiment. "Our lab exercise for those who want: try out a free text-to-speech tool. Type a paragraph of something, maybe an excerpt from your last report, and see how it sounds read by an AI voice. If you find a platform with avatars, give that a go too. It's a bit of a rabbit hole because you'll end up trying all the different voice styles. But it's important to understand the capabilities and limitations first-hand."

As class ended, Alex chatted virtually with a couple of fellow attendees about the possibilities. Jordan said his company was thinking of using AI voices for their phone customer service line. "It's gotten good enough that callers might not even know," he said. "As long as it's clear and helpful, why not?"

Before signing off, Tasha pinged him. "Are you going to try making a video for your team, Alex?" she asked.

"Actually, yes," Alex replied. "I'm already thinking about an internal training video we could do. Maybe a quick one on our new project management tool, with an AI narrator. It could save us doing a live demo over and over."

Tasha nodded enthusiastically. "I'm thinking about doing the same for my team. I'd love to share notes with you and maybe we can learn from each other!."

"Yeah, that sounds great. The more experience the better!" Alex typed, and added a 'strong' emoji.

Back at work the next day, Alex couldn't wait to experiment while the experience was fresh. During his lunch break, he drafted a short script for a one-minute internal video introducing the concept of AI avatars. It was meta: a video about AI tools, made with AI tools. The script read like a friendly announcement: "Hello team, in this video we want to show you a new way we can create training content more efficiently..." and so on.

He signed up for a trial on one of the AI avatar platforms Blaze mentioned. The interface let him choose from several presenter avatars. He chose one that looked like a clean-cut young professional man with a warm demeanor, figuring that would be broadly appealing. He also selected a voice, a pleasant baritone that sounded natural.

After pasting in his script and selecting a background color with the company logo, Alex hit "Generate." The website began assembling the video. In a couple of minutes, it was ready. Alex clicked play and watched with a mixture of excitement and nervousness.

There was "Nick," the AI presenter, smiling and looking into the camera. "Hello team," Nick said in a confident voice, "I'm here to demonstrate how AI can help us create training content more efficiently..." As the avatar spoke the words Alex had written, Alex felt a surreal pride. This digital presenter was essentially acting as his stand-in.

He did notice a few quirks: a mispronounced acronym (AI voices often stumble over certain abbreviations) and a slight stiffness in a head movement. But overall, it looked really good for something produced by a computer in minutes.

Alex showed the video to Priya and Robert that afternoon. Priya was astonished. "I thought that was a real guy, like an actor you hired, until I realized the voice was exactly following the script text you shared. This is wild."

Robert joked, "Can we create a virtual version of me to give all my status updates? Imagine, I could be on the beach while my Avatar runs the meetings." Alex laughed, "One day, maybe. But we'd know it wasn't really you, Robert, the jokes would be better."

They all laughed, and then agreed the technology had real potential. Priya said, "For our new hire orientations, we could make a series of these so everyone gets the same training content without scheduling live sessions each time."

"Exactly," Alex said, glad his team was seeing the practical value. "And we should definitely note in the video or at the end that it was AI-generated, so people aren't confused or misled."

Robert nodded, "Yeah, transparency is key. We don't want anyone thinking we're trying to trick them. Plus, internally, it's kind of cool to say we made this with AI."

Buoyed by the positive reaction, Alex and his colleagues decided to propose a pilot project to create a set of internal training videos with AI narration. Alex volunteered to draft a brief for their manager, explaining the idea and the expected benefits. He felt confident he could make a strong case, especially armed with what he learned from Blaze, the cost savings, the speed, and examples of other companies doing the same.

That evening at home, Alex couldn't resist sharing his AI video with Maria and Sophie. He played it on the living room TV. As the virtual presenter "Nick" appeared and spoke, Sophie's eyes went wide.

"That's not a real person, is it?" she asked, getting up from the couch to walk closer to the screen. She studied the avatar's face intently.

"Nope, he's completely AI," Alex said, pleased at her reaction. "I made this today using an AI avatar tool. What do you think?"

Sophie tilted her head. "He looks real at first, but... I don't know. There's something about the eyes and the way he pauses that feels a tiny bit unnatural. It's kind of cool but also a bit creepy."

Maria chimed in, "If you hadn't told me, I might not realize. But since I know, I keep trying to spot the flaws. The voice is almost too consistent, if that makes sense. People usually say 'um' or have a bit more emotion."

"True," Alex agreed. "The AI doesn't do little imperfections unless you program it to. It comes off as very polished, which can sound robotic in its own way."

Sophie nodded vigorously. "Yeah. It's like how animated characters in older video games looked almost real but you *knew* they weren't. This is much better than that, but it still doesn't feel alive to me."

"That's the trade-off," Alex said. "It's an amazing tool for certain uses, but it won't replace a genuine human connection when you need that. Like, I wouldn't use an avatar to give a heartfelt message or anything."

Maria smiled, "I should hope not. If you ever send an AI avatar to deliver our anniversary message, we're going to have a problem."

Alex laughed and raised his hands in surrender. "Never, I promise. Only genuine me for that."

As they settled in for the night, Alex opened his notebook to jot a couple of key insights from the day:

> AI voices and avatars save time and money, but authenticity and honesty matter.

Always disclose AI-generated media, trust is more important than tech magic.

He underlined "trust" for emphasis. Closing his notebook, Alex felt a growing sense of responsibility. He was becoming the de facto AI ambassador among his peers and family, and it was important to lead by example. The tools were powerful, now it was about using them in a way that felt right.

Tomorrow, Blaze's session would shift to using AI for strategy and growth. Alex was eager to see how the bootcamp would tie everything together, from the creative side into big-picture thinking. He headed to bed, mind buzzing with ideas of what else could be possible.

Chapter 14: Strategy and Growth

Alex logged into the virtual bootcamp classroom with a fresh cup of coffee and a sense of purpose. Today's session promised to be a big one, tying together everything they'd learned, but at a higher level. The title popped up:

AI for Strategy and Growth

Blaze greeted the class and jumped right in. "We've talked about using AI for writing, data, code, visuals, voice… What about using it to actually guide our decisions and plans? Today is about using AI as a thinking partner for strategy."

He began by asking, "How do you usually start when you're faced with a big project or a tough problem?" People offered answers: "Brainstorm ideas," "Do research," "Outline options," "Get feedback." Blaze nodded. "Those are exactly the kinds of tasks AI can assist with. Think of it as a sounding board that has read everything and doesn't run out of ideas."

Blaze outlined several strategic uses for AI:

- Brainstorming: "Whether you need a list of campaign ideas or product features, tools like ChatGPT can spit out dozens of suggestions in seconds. Some will be junk, sure, but even one good idea can justify the effort. And it can help you think outside your usual box by injecting fresh perspectives."

- Outlining and organizing: "If you're not sure how to structure a plan or proposal, ask AI to draft an outline. It's great at taking a vague prompt like 'marketing plan for product launch' and giving you a skeleton to start with. You can then fill in details and rearrange as needed."

- Scenario planning: "AI can help simulate 'what if' scenarios. For example, you can prompt it with, 'Imagine the market grows 20% next year, how should our strategy adapt?' and it will narrate an answer. It's surprisingly good at exploring hypothetical situations, which helps you anticipate outcomes. This is essentially a way to stress-test your plans against different assumptions."

- Role-playing: "Need to prepare for a negotiation or an interview? You can have the AI act as the other party. Say you have a difficult customer situation, you can role-play with ChatGPT acting as the customer to practice your responses. Or if you're going into a job interview, have it pose common interview questions. It can simulate a mock interview and even give you feedback on your answers."

- Decision support: "Having trouble weighing options? Ask the AI to list pros and cons, or to perform a SWOT analysis (strengths, weaknesses, opportunities, threats) for a situation. It can analyze a scenario and highlight factors to consider, sometimes pointing out things you might miss. Just remember it's not magical truth, you still have to apply your own judgment."

Alex wrote in his notebook:

> AI = brainstorming buddy and scenario simulator.

Blaze then gave a live demonstration. He set up a quick role-play in his chat and told the AI to act as a skeptical manager in a raise negotiation. The AI obliged with a tough question, and after Blaze responded, it followed up with a pointed critique that he hadn't mentioned some of his recent successes, exactly the kind of feedback a real boss might give.

"See that?" Blaze said, pointing at the chat exchange on screen. "It zeroed in on something I forgot to mention. This is like having a colleague or coach available anytime to practice difficult conversations. It's a confidence booster."

He did note a caution: "Now, remember, AI can also produce bad advice or incorrect information, especially if you ask it very factual strategic questions. Always double-check important facts and don't blindly follow AI's suggestions. Use it to amplify your thinking, not replace it. Think of it as an intern with encyclopedic knowledge but not much wisdom. It needs guidance."

The class chuckled at that analogy, and Alex found it very apt.

As Blaze wrapped up the lecture portion, he said, "Alright, let's talk about how you all can apply this. Who has a project or decision where they might try using AI to help?"

Alex felt his hand rising before he even fully processed, this was his moment. "I'm part of our company's working group for rolling out AI tools," he said. "One thing we need is a strategic plan for a phased rollout. I was thinking of using AI to help outline that plan."

Blaze beamed. "Perfect example. Using AI to plan how to use AI, I love it. Why don't you share how you approach that with the group next time? Actually, let's workshop it a bit now."

Alex described the general goal: "We want a roadmap for introducing AI in our operations over, say, the next year or two, in stages. There are many angles, training staff, setting policies, choosing pilot projects, scaling up usage, and so on. It's a lot to organize."

Blaze turned that into a prompt for the class: "What could Alex ask the AI to get started on this plan?"

"Maybe: 'Outline a phased implementation plan for adopting AI in a mid-size company'?" Mia suggested.

"Good," Blaze said, typing that into the chat. The AI responded with a structured multi-phase plan. It suggested starting with a pilot and task force, providing training and creating guidelines, next scaling up successful pilots, followed by refining and optimizing, and finally committing to continuous improvement. It attached timelines to each phase.

Alex's eyes lit up as he read the AI's answer. This was exactly the sort of structure he had been envisioning, but seeing it neatly laid out was incredibly helpful. "This is great," Alex said. "It basically confirms and organizes what I had in mind, and even adds points I hadn't explicitly thought of yet."

Blaze nodded. "Notice how the AI came up with sensible phases that cover everything from initial pilots to long-term improvement. It's like a consultant giving a first draft. Alex will need to adjust this to fit his company's context, maybe the timelines change, maybe they'll add a step about choosing the right software, but it's a solid starting framework."

Alex quickly jotted in his notes:

Phased AI rollout: Pilot → Train → Scale → Optimize → Evolve.

Blaze reminded everyone, "Using AI for strategic thinking doesn't absolve you from thinking. It just gives you more angles and data to consider. Always align the AI's input with your real-world context and goals, and verify anything that seems uncertain."

After class, Alex felt a surge of motivation. He had the outline, and he was determined to flesh it out and present it to his company's working group.

Over the next few days at work, Alex dedicated time to develop the AI rollout plan. He used the AI-generated outline as a base and expanded each section with specifics. Whenever he got stuck or wanted more ideas, he turned to ChatGPT with targeted prompts:

- He asked, "What potential risks might we face in Phase 3 (Scaling AI) and how can we mitigate them?" The AI suggested issues like employee resistance or data privacy concerns, and offered mitigation ideas (like change management communications and strict compliance checks) that Alex incorporated.

- He prompted, "Give some metrics to track AI adoption success." It came back with suggestions: productivity improvement percentages, employee AI tool usage rates, cost savings, error reduction. Alex picked a few that made sense and added a section on key performance indicators.

- For an executive summary, he even asked, "Help draft a short summary of this plan to share with leadership." The AI produced a neat paragraph highlighting the plan's goals and phases, which Alex tweaked and used at the top of his document.

Each time, Alex was careful to review the AI's suggestions. Sometimes it proposed something that wouldn't work at his company (like a tool they didn't use), so he adjusted or omitted those bits. It was truly a collaborative process: human experience and AI's breadth of knowledge working together.

One evening, as Alex was polishing the final draft at home, Maria walked by the dining table where he had his notes sprawled out. "Wow, that's a lot of writing. What are you working on?"

"Believe it or not, this is the AI strategy plan for work," he said, leaning back. "I've been using ChatGPT to help me brainstorm and organize it."

Maria peered at his notebook and laptop. "You're using AI to plan AI? That's kinda meta," she teased.

"Totally meta," Alex laughed. "But it's been a huge help. For instance, I wasn't sure how to approach the training section, so I asked for some ideas, and it gave me a few good ones that I adapted."

Maria pulled up a chair, interested. "Maybe it can help me too… I'm trying to map out a marketing calendar for my candles for the next few months. Like, what themes or promotions to do each month. I have some ideas but I wonder if it could spark something."

"Let's try it," Alex said, happy to take a little break from his own work. He opened a new chat and prompted: "Suggest a month-by-month marketing theme or promotion for a small business selling handmade candles and aromatherapy products."

Within moments, the AI replied with a month-by-month list of ideas, from a "New Year, Fresh Scents" theme in January, to Valentine's gift sets in February, spring renewal ideas in March, a self-care promotion in April, all the way through holiday special suggestions at year-end.

"This is amazing!" Maria said, grabbing a pen to jot down a few favorites. "It even remembered things like Mother's Day in May, I didn't think of that. And the 'Home Spa Day' idea in April for stress awareness, that's clever."

Alex smiled, watching Maria get inspired. "The AI is like having a marketing assistant brainstorming with you."

"Of course, I'll still need to actually create the content and make sure these ideas fit my brand," Maria noted, "but this is a fantastic starting point. It definitely saved me hours of staring at a blank calendar."

She paused and added, "I'll double-check any dates or facts it gave, just to be safe."

"Good plan," Alex agreed. Blaze's voice in his head would never let him forget to verify.

With Maria's calendar sketched out, Alex returned to his strategy document. It was nearly ready for prime time. The working group meeting to review the plan was scheduled for next week, and he was both anxious and excited.

He would have preferred to complete the boot camp before giving this critical presentation, just to ensure he had learned as much as possible. But the final session was the following week and was mostly a recap of lessons learned in the first 5 sessions, with participants demonstrating what they had learned. At least he'd already had 5 productive sessions with Blaze and was feeling pretty confident.

On the day of the presentation, Alex walked into the conference room with printouts of the rollout plan and a PowerPoint deck he had prepared (with a little AI assistance on formatting and proofreading, naturally). The audience consisted of Alex's working group members, department heads and a couple of C-suite executives, including the CTO who served as the corporate sponsor of the AI initiative. As the AI working group lead, Alex was tasked with convincing the higher ups in the company that his strategy was going to get them where they wanted to go.

Alex kicked off the meeting. "Thanks everyone for being here. I'm excited to share a draft of our AI rollout strategy." He felt a familiar flutter of nerves, but also confidence from his thorough preparation. As he began walking through the slides, outlining each phase of the plan, he found his rhythm.

He explained Phase 1: Small pilot projects and assembling an AI task force. There were nods around the table. They'd already identified a couple of pilot ideas, so this resonated.

Phase 2: Training and guidelines. The HR director smiled at the emphasis on upskilling employees and having ethical use policies. Alex mentioned, "We should establish clear guidelines for responsible AI use, so everyone knows the dos and don'ts," reflecting Blaze's lessons.

He continued to Phase 3: Scaling successful pilots. Vanessa Juarez, the Chief Technology Officer (CTO), chimed in, "We'll want to track results from the pilots before a broad rollout," which segued perfectly into Alex's next slide.

Phase 4: Optimization. This is where we tighten up what we have built so far and fix any issues that surface. And lastly, Phase 5: Continuous Improvement. We'll establish an AI steering committee to guide updates, evaluate new tools, and help us continue learning and improving over time.

Vanessa smiled. "Alex, this is an excellent framework. It's clear you put a lot of thought into it." Another executive agreed, noting the phased approach showed exactly the kind of foresight they needed.

A few questions came up about timelines and tool choices. Alex explained that phases might overlap naturally and assured them the specifics of tools and vendors would be fleshed out as the plan progressed. Overall, the plan was very well received.

Vanessa concluded, "Let's use this draft to move forward. We'll refine responsibilities and deliverables under each phase, but I think we have our roadmap. Great work, Alex. And team, this is the kind of forward-thinking approach we need. We should all leverage these tools and insights to stay ahead."

Alex felt a surge of pride. In that moment, he decided to be completely transparent. "I have a little confession about how I put this together," he said, half-smiling. The room looked at him curiously. "I used ChatGPT to help me brainstorm and structure the plan. I obviously customized and edited the heck out of it, but it definitely accelerated my work."

There was a brief silence, and then Vanessa laughed, "Well, that's fitting, isn't it? Using AI to help craft our AI strategy." A few others chuckled and nodded in agreement. One manager said, "Honestly, that's great to hear. We should probably all be doing that more."

With that, the meeting wrapped up on a high note.

Later that day, Alex met up with Mark to tell him how the presentation went. Mark congratulated him warmly, then said, "Actually, I have some news, I landed an interview for a new role next week. It's with a company looking for people who understand how AI can improve operations."

"That's fantastic, Mark!" Alex replied. Noticing that Mark was excited but a little nervous, he added, "Do you want to practice? We could do a mock interview this weekend and even have ChatGPT throw some tough questions at you."

Mark's face lit up. "You read my mind. I could definitely use the practice."

"You got it," Alex said with a grin. "We'll make sure you go in confident and prepared."

That night, Alex reflected on the whirlwind of the past few weeks. He had transformed from someone apprehensive about AI into someone leading AI initiatives and helping others adapt. Blaze's bootcamp had been the catalyst, but it was Alex's own openness to learn and try things (and a bit of late-night practice with ChatGPT) that had gotten him here.

In his notebook, he wrote one last bold reminder to himself:

> Stay adaptive and keep learning, the journey never really ends.

He closed the notebook with a smile. There would always be new changes and challenges, but he felt ready to face them. With AI as an ally, he was confident he could continue to adapt and thrive as a true adaptive professional.

Chapter 15: Adaptive Action Plan

Blaze sat in front of his webcam with a warm smile. "Good evening, everyone! I can hardly believe this is our last session." One by one, faces appeared on the screen. Alex was leaning back in his chair, the late-evening light behind him. Tasha sat with a notebook, pen in hand. Mia waved from her home office, and Jordan gave a thumbs-up. The video call gallery was like a patchwork quilt of smiling faces, and everyone seemed to sense the occasion.

Tasha stretched and grinned. "It's crazy how fast it went. Remember when I said AI would replace teachers in our first class?"

Everyone laughed. Blaze nodded. "And now look at you, using ChatGPT to help craft your lesson plans instead of fearing it."

Alex chuckled. "Back in session one, I was *really* nervous about this AI stuff. I thought I'd be out of a job by next week."

Blaze raised an eyebrow playfully. "Oh, you and a lot of others felt that way. What changed for you?"

Alex smiled thoughtfully. "You guys showed me it's not some magic boogeyman. It's a tool. This bootcamp helped me see that I can use AI to do my job better, like making me twice as efficient, not irrelevant."

"That's the spirit," Blaze said. "Tasha, you jumped right in too. How do you feel now?"

Tasha beamed. "Honestly? Empowered. After using AI to draft letters, summarize articles, even prepare for meetings, I feel like I'm the one in control. I know now how to manage the tech, not the other way around."

Mia nodded. "I was the skeptical newbie, but now I'm telling all my coworkers about these tools."

Jordan added, "Same here. It feels good to speak up when others complain about AI. I can say, hey, I learned how to use it. It's actually pretty cool."

Blaze laughed. "That's what I like to hear: confidence and curiosity. Tonight, let's talk about the future: how to keep this going," he continued. "I've put together a framework to help you apply everything you've learned once this course ends." He brought up his title slide and exclaimed, "let's jump in!"

Adaptive Action Plan

Everyone leaned in as Blaze shared his screen with a whiteboard filled with notes. "Think of the Adaptive Action Plan as your personal roadmap. It's not one-size-fits-all, each of you will adapt it to your goals and work. Let's go through the key steps together."

Blaze clicked through slides and listed the plan steps:

1. **Clarify Your Vision and Values:** Define what you want to achieve. Think about your purpose and what motivates you. For example, Alex said he wants to make his marketing more creative and data-driven. That's his

vision. Tasha's vision might be helping students learn better. Keep that in mind at every step.

2. **Inventory Your Tasks and Skills:** List your regular tasks and see which could be enhanced by AI. Identify the skills or tools you need. Tasha, you write lesson plans and emails, AI can help draft those. And Alex, you mentioned analyzing customer feedback used to take forever. Now you can paste comments into your AI assistant and instantly see the overall tone, what people liked, what frustrated them, and the big themes. That's called sentiment analysis, and it saves hours.

3. **Set Small Experiments:** Pick one area to try first. Don't try to change everything overnight. For example, write one newsletter email with your AI assistant and see how it goes. Make it a fun test with a short deadline. It doesn't have to be perfect the first time.

4. **Gather Feedback and Reflect:** After your experiment, show the results to a colleague or friend. Ask if it was helpful and compare it to how you did it before. Note what worked well and what didn't. Reflection is key to learning.

5. **Iterate and Adapt:** Use what you learned to tweak your approach. If the result wasn't quite right, adjust the prompts or try a different tool. Keep looping through "Try → Reflect → Adjust." Over time, you'll find a better way of working. As things change, you can update the plan.

6. **Collaborate and Share:** Join communities or talk with peers. Share what you've learned, like successful prompts or tips. Reading how others solved problems (our Slack channel, for example, Facebook groups, or group chats) can give you ideas and keep you motivated.

7. **Stay Human-Centric:** Above all, keep empathy, ethics, and creativity at the center of your work. Use AI to enhance your uniquely human strengths. Always ask: How does this serve people better?

Blaze smiled. "The Adaptive Action Plan isn't just a checklist, it's a mindset. You can write these steps down and really use them as a guide. Adjust as you go."

He sat back. "Now, let's make this real. Alex, what's one thing you want to focus on after tonight? How would you apply this plan in your work?"

Alex thought a moment. "My biggest goal is to improve our client reporting process. Using the plan: I already have my goal. For tasks, I listed things like reviewing and summarizing data, writing clear and effective reports with appropriate and informative graphics. I realize AI can help with much of this. For a small test, I'll use ChatGPT on my next report and see if it speeds things up without losing quality."

Tasha chimed in, "And then in feedback, Alex, you'd compare the AI outline to what you normally do and ask your team if it hits the mark."

"Exactly," Alex said. "Then I'd iterate, if it's not quite right, tweak the prompt or approach. I'd let the team know what I learned so we all improve. And through it all, I keep our brand voice human."

Blaze beamed. "Nice example! You've already done something like this before. Now it's just part of your plan." Tasha laughed. "Blaze, you should take notes! I think we have this on record."

Alex grinned. "Well, I learned from the best."

Blaze turned to Tasha. "How about you, Tasha? What will you do first with the plan?"

Tasha tapped her pen. "I want to tackle my monthly reports. I spend two evenings formatting and summarizing. For a small test, I'll have ChatGPT draft the summaries. Then I'll ask my team lead if the draft captured the key points and refine it from there. That way I save time and can use it to connect more with the students."

"That's a smart approach," Blaze said. "It's helping you focus on what you care about most."

Mia shared quickly, "I'm going to use AI to help write captions for social media and see what feedback I get from our audience."

Jordan smiled. "And I'm going to use my AI assistant to help with my grocery list," (he laughed) "just kidding. But seriously, I'll pick one mundane task at a time and try automating it."

The discussion hummed with energy as participants jumped in with ideas. Blaze prompted gently, tying their examples back to the plan steps.

"And recall," he interjected, "that we've been talking a lot about ChatGPT, which is a highly versatile AI assistant. But remember that there are many similar AI assistants (or chatbots) including: Claude (by Anthropic), Google's Gemini, and Microsoft Copilot, as a few examples, with new platforms emerging every few months."

Finally, Blaze brought everyone's attention back. "You all have solid starting points. The plan is flexible, it might look different for each of you, and that's perfect. The key is to keep practicing over time. Now, let's talk about one more thing: what's next after tonight?"

The tone turned warmly reflective. Alex said, "Honestly, I'm leaving tonight feeling really excited. I've got a clear path for what I'll do next at work. I'm even a bit proud of myself, thanks to all of you, I feel ready to bring these ideas up instead of hiding."

Tasha nodded. "Same here. Before I joined, I was worried about how I would cope with AI. Now I feel like I can actually lead with it. I'm not just hoping for the best; I have a plan."

Mia chimed in, "This has been life-changing. I'll keep checking our Slack to help others the way I was helped."

Jordan smiled. "Me too. By the way, does this mean we stop meeting? Because I'd love more."

Blaze nodded. "We will always be a community. The Slack channel stays open. And speaking of more stories, Alex, you mentioned your colleague Robert the other day. Tell everyone about him?"

Alex tilted his camera, a playful grin on his face. "Oh, Robert. He's been in marketing for, like, twenty years. He was completely freaked out when AI started taking over simple tasks. He even called me last week feeling useless. But I told him about our bootcamp and he tried using ChatGPT to streamline his reports, and suddenly he had more time for strategy. He ended up reinvigorating his career, feeling like he reinvented himself."

Blaze's eyes lit up. "That's an inspiring story. Robert took that same plan and turned his fear into an opportunity, just like all of you have already."

Alex smiled. "I guess we *all* have come a long way!."

Blaze nodded and closed the discussion warmly. "I'm so proud of all of you. Keep using your Adaptive Action Plans, keep in touch, and remember, your human qualities are what make all of this work. Use AI as your co-pilot, not the driver. Alex and Tasha, I can see how much you've grown. I'm excited to see where you all go from here."

With that, the participants took turns signing off. They thanked Blaze, congratulated each other, and even ended with a quick group photo screenshot with virtual hats on, courtesy of a final chat sticker. Smiles and cheers faded as the call ended.

Blaze sat back with a satisfied smile. In his mind he was already picturing the next story, the reinvention of Robert, which would be the perfect example of this plan in action. But for now, tonight's bootcamp chapter had reached a joyful close.

Alex closed his laptop feeling confident, hopeful, and ready for what came next. Everyone left the call on a high note, carrying the empowerment of the bootcamp and the promise of new adventures ahead.

Chapter 16: Robert's Reinvention

Alex paused in the doorway of the accounting department's small conference room. Inside, Robert was hunched over his laptop, two spreadsheets and a text editor open on the screen. For the past two decades, Robert had been the firm's go-to expert on complex reconciliations, the process of matching accounts and records until everything lined up just right. He was known for doing things methodically and by the book, often printing out ledgers to mark them with a red pen. But today, something was different.

"Let's see what you make of this," Robert murmured to his computer, almost as if coaching it along. Alex stepped closer and realized Robert wasn't talking to himself, he was guiding an AI tool through a tricky reconciliation problem. Rows of figures scrolled by as Robert fed prompts and commands, and the AI highlighted mismatches and proposed adjustments in real-time.

Alex couldn't help but smile. He gently knocked on the door frame. "Burning the midnight oil, Robert? Or should I say, training your new helper?" he asked warmly.

Robert looked up, eyes twinkling behind his glasses. "Caught me in the act," he said with a sheepish grin. "Old dogs and new tricks, right?"

Alex stepped into the room and set his coffee mug down. "If this is what an old dog can do, then I think the rest of us pups better pay attention."

Robert leaned back, stretching his shoulders. On the screen, the AI had flagged a list of transactions that didn't match between the company's general ledger and bank statements.

Normally, Robert would comb through these line by line, a tedious process sometimes taking days. Now, his custom script had reduced it to a couple of hours. "I was skeptical at first," Robert admitted, "but with what you shared with the group last week about AI tools for automating grunt work I saw potential. I've been tinkering with it on my own ever since, with guidance from ChatGPT."

Alex said, nodding. "You asked some really sharp questions during the Q&A. Honestly, I'm impressed you ran with it."

Robert chuckled and rubbed the back of his neck. "Well, I figured I should try it out on something low-stakes first, just some internal reconciling for a smaller client. I built a little workflow to feed the data in, let the AI suggest matches, and then I manually review each suggestion." He pointed to a step-by-step list he'd written on a notepad by his laptop. Each step was numbered and annotated in Robert's neat handwriting. "This is my cheat sheet," he said. "Keeps me from getting lost."

Alex picked up the notepad and scanned it. It was a detailed checklist:

1. Upload data to AI tool.
2. Run initial reconciliation suggestions.
3. Cross-verify flagged items against source documents.
4. Document any AI-proposed adjustments.
5. Manually approve and finalize the reconciled accounts.

It was classic Robert, thorough and systematic. He had effectively created a human-AI collaboration workflow where the AI did the heavy lifting but every critical judgment still passed through Robert's seasoned eyes. "This is fantastic," Alex said sincerely. "It's like you've turned the AI into your junior analyst, one that works at lightning speed."

"Exactly," Robert replied. He tapped the laptop screen, where a particularly nasty discrepancy was highlighted in yellow. "See this? The AI spotted that an invoice was recorded twice under slightly different reference numbers. I might have caught it eventually, but it saved me at least an hour of digging. Of course, I still verified it was indeed a duplicate before adjusting the entry. Trust, but verify, that's my motto with these things."

Alex nodded vigorously. "And that's exactly what the firm's guidance suggests too. Use the AI to assist, but always review its output. You've basically crafted a model example of responsible AI use."

They shared a brief moment of satisfaction, marveling at the reconciliation now balanced to the penny. Alex felt a surge of pride in Robert's accomplishment. It wasn't just that Robert had saved time; it was that he had done it by blending decades of experience with brand-new technology. The wisdom of his practice was now augmented by AI, not replaced by it.

"Have you shown anyone else on the team this workflow?" Alex asked, thinking of the potential impact if others adopted it.

"Not formally," Robert said. "I've mentioned bits and pieces in passing. I helped Jenna last week when she was struggling with a tax memo. We used a similar approach, I had her draft the memo then run sections through the AI for clarity and additional citations. She was amazed at how it suggested phrasing to make the complex tax regulation sound straightforward. But she still reviewed every line to make sure it was accurate and fit our tone. We turned a dense five-page memo into a crisp three-page brief that a client could actually understand."

Alex's eyebrows rose. He hadn't heard about that success yet. Jenna was a younger associate, tech-savvy herself, and probably one of the few people Robert would quietly mentor. "That's a big win. Did the client read it?"

Robert chuckled. "Not only read it, apparently he thanked Jenna for writing something 'finally understandable'. That made her day. Made mine too, to see her feeling proud rather than drained by that task."

Alex felt a familiar excitement growing, that spark when you realize you're onto something that could help many. He and Robert had both been collecting little victories with these AI tools, and it was time to connect the dots. "Robert," Alex said thoughtfully, "I think we should share what's working. Firm-wide."

Robert tilted his head. "You mean, like a training or a memo?"

"Maybe more. We could propose adding these methods to the official AI Use Guidelines." Alex began pacing slowly, organizing thoughts aloud. "The firm rolled out broad guidelines after my presentation to corporate, mostly principles about confidentiality, verification, and not relying on AI for final sign-off. But they were generic. What you've developed here are specific, battle-tested practices: a reconciliation workflow, an approach for tax memos. If we formalize these, we give everyone a head start. We turn what you and Jenna did into standard practice."

Robert's eyes lit up, then he furrowed his brow in concern. "Do you think Vanessa would go for that? I mean, I'm all for it, but they might say it's too early or want to pilot it quietly."

"That's why we frame it carefully," Alex replied, warming to the idea. "We highlight the benefits, saved time, better accuracy, happier clients. And we show that it doesn't replace professional judgment, it enhances it. Coming from you, someone with 35 years of client trust, it'll carry weight. It shows that this isn't a fad, it's a genuine improvement in how we work."

Robert slowly nodded, a smile creeping back. "It would be something, to contribute to the firm in a new way like this. After so long, you think you've settled into your role. But here we are, I'm learning from the new and pairing it with the old." He tapped his pen on the notepad thoughtfully. "Alright. Let's do it. Let's draft a proposal."

They decided to work on it first thing in the morning.

The next day, Alex and Robert gathered their notes and met in a small conference room that Alex jokingly called "the lab". Alex brought his laptop, Robert brought a stack of printouts and his notepad.

Together, they outlined the proposal:

- Introduction: A recap of the firm's current AI guidelines and the purpose of the proposal, emphasizing building on what's already in place.

- Success Stories: Robert described the reconciliation case study and the tax memo case. Alex helped put the narrative into a concise write-up, highlighting time saved and positive feedback from the client on the memo.

- Proposed Workflow Additions: Step-by-step recommended practices for using AI in reconciliations (Robert's checklist) and for drafting tax memos (like an outline, AI-assisted clarity pass, then human review).

- Benefits: More efficient processes, more consistent quality, and mentorship opportunities (pairing less experienced staff with veterans like Robert to learn these workflows).

- Safeguards: A section reinforcing that AI suggestions must be verified, data privacy must be maintained (no feeding sensitive client data into outside tools without approval), and human judgment remains key.

As they wrote, their roles naturally fell into place. Alex typed and structured the document, choosing words carefully. Robert paced and dictated some lines, occasionally leaning over Alex's shoulder to point out where a detail could be clearer. At one point, Alex suggested they have an AI tool read over their draft to catch any unclear language. "Using AI to write our AI guidelines proposal… I guess this is where the future is heading," he joked.

By late afternoon, they had a solid draft. Alex sent it to a few colleagues for feedback: Jenna, of course, and also Priya, who had been championing the original guidelines, and Marcus, a partner known for being forward-thinking. They wanted allies on board before presenting it formally.

Within a day, feedback trickled in. Jenna wrote back first, enthusiastic: the proposal was clear and she loved that her tax memo story was included (she even sent along a quote from the happy client email, which Alex added verbatim to the proposal). Priya added some suggestions on aligning it with the firm's tone and reminded them to mention compliance had vetted the AI tools being used. Marcus's reply came with a short note: "This is excellent. Let's discuss at the department head meeting."

And so, a week later, Alex and Robert found themselves in the glass-walled boardroom on the 20th floor, presenting "AI Guidelines Update Proposal" to a small group of firm leaders. Alex felt a slight nervous flutter, these meetings could be formal, but he reminded himself that the content was solid and Robert's presence was an anchor of credibility.

Robert, in his element, spoke calmly as he described how he used the AI for reconciliations. There was a subtle shift in the room's energy as some senior managers, who likely hadn't tried these tools firsthand, leaned forward in interest. When Robert recounted the duplicate invoice the AI identified in seconds, Alex saw nods and raised eyebrows. It was the kind of efficiency everyone in the industry dreamed of, but hearing it from Robert made it tangible.

Alex then walked through the written proposal projected on the screen. He pointed out the new step-by-step workflows they were recommending and how they dovetailed with existing procedures. Priya, who was in attendance, chimed in to mention the training angle: "This allows our experienced folks to mentor the younger ones in a new way. Instead of keeping AI experimentation siloed, we're turning it into shared knowledge."

One of the more traditional partners, Elaine, tapped her pen and asked, "This all sounds good, but what about quality control? Are we confident that these AI suggestions won't introduce errors that a human might miss?"

Robert took that one. "Elaine, I had the same concern. That's why in these workflows, the AI is a first pass, not the final word. Think of it as having an extra pair of eyes that never get tired of cross-checking. I still review each reconciliation item. In fact, in my trial runs, I caught the AI incorrectly matching something once or twice, and that's noted in the proposal. Our policy remains that a certified professional signs off. So this doesn't remove oversight; it improves it by focusing our attention where it's needed."

Elaine seemed satisfied, and Marcus added, "And by sharing Robert's process, we ensure others won't just blindly trust the AI either. They'll follow his lead, trust but verify."

The discussion continued for a few more minutes. A question about compliance came up: Priya responded that they were using approved tools and that part of the proposal included a reminder of data guidelines. Another question was about training time: Alex pointed out that since Robert's methods were documented clearly, it could be integrated into upcoming training with minimal fuss.

Finally, Vanessa, who had been quiet so far, cleared her throat. "This is excellent work," she said in a measured tone. "What I find most heartening is that it comes from within our ranks, and from one of our most seasoned professionals, no less." She offered Robert a respectful nod. "It shows that innovation isn't just the domain of the new hires or tech specialists; it's everyone's business. Let's move forward with this. Priya, work with Alex and Robert to finalize the updated guidelines, and we'll circulate firm-wide next month."

Alex exhaled, realizing he'd been holding his breath for that response. A grin broke out on Robert's face. They had done it. Their proposal was officially adopted.

On the way out of the boardroom, as attendees dispersed, Marcus clapped Robert on the back. "You know, if you ever get tired of reconciliations, you might have a second career in process innovation," he quipped.

Robert laughed. "At my age? I think I'll stick to what I know a little while longer. But it does feel good to shake things up, I admit."

Alex walked with Robert to the elevator lobby, feeling a deep sense of satisfaction. "Robert, I'm really happy for you, for us," Alex said. "This will make a difference to so many people's day-to-day work. And you led the charge."

Robert smiled, a bit emotionally. "I have to thank you too, Alex. You gave me the push and the platform. I probably would have just kept tinkering quietly if you hadn't suggested making it a firm initiative. It reminds me of something I wrote down in my notebook the day after one of your earlier presentations."

He paused as they waited for the elevator. Alex tilted his head curiously. "What did you write?"

Robert looked slightly embarrassed but then, seeing Alex's genuine interest, he answered: "I wrote: *Never too old to adapt. Experience has value, but only if I'm willing to learn something new.* I guess this old dog took that to heart, huh?"

The elevator arrived with a soft ding. Alex placed a hand on Robert's shoulder as they stepped in. "I'd say you did. And we're all better for it."

As the doors closed, Alex thought of the journey they had taken over the past year, from initial skepticism and learning to concrete change and improvement. He resolved to jot down his own reflections later, mindful of how far they'd come.

Even the most experienced professionals can reinvent themselves. Today I saw how wisdom and openness together spark innovation. Sharing Robert's method with the firm proved that when we value each other's strengths and styles, everyone moves forward.

Chapter 17: The Client Advantage

A week later, Alex found himself straightening a stack of printouts and adjusting the projector in a client's boardroom. This time, it wasn't an internal meeting, it was the big presentation for Barnwell Retail, one of the firm's longstanding regional clients. The room smelled of fresh coffee and anticipation as Alex's team prepared to present their annual financial analysis.

Jenna clicked through the slides on the laptop, doing a final check. On the screen was a title page with the firm's logo and, in bold, a simple title: Barnwell Retail: 2025 Performance Review, Key Insights. It was a far cry from the jargon-heavy titles of past years. The content was equally transformed, concise summaries, easy-to-read charts, and even a few illustrated scenarios showing trends in customer behavior. Much of this polish was thanks to AI assistance, and the team was both excited and a little nervous to see how the client would react.

Alex glanced at his two colleagues: Jenna, who'd taken the lead on creating visuals, and Martin, a senior analyst who had crunched the numbers. Both were younger than him and brimming with tech skills, but this was the first time they'd so heavily leaned on AI for a client deliverable. Jenna had used an AI tool to generate icons and color-coded charts that made the data pop. Martin had run the dense financial tables through an AI summarizer to pull out key patterns in sales and expenses, which they then turned into a one-page executive summary.

"Slide 5, the cash flow diagram, looks great," Jenna said, glancing at Alex. "I still can't believe that graphic was created from my rough sketch by an AI in like, two minutes."

Alex smiled. "It does look great, and it illustrates the point immediately. Remember last year's report? We had a wall of numbers on cash flow. This is going to be so much clearer."

Martin, hovering by the conference phone to dial in a remote client executive, chimed in with a hint of worry. "I hope 'clearer' doesn't come off as 'dumbed down'. We've got all the detailed schedules in the appendix, but the main deck is... well, it's pretty high-level compared to what we used to do."

Alex walked over and patted Martin on the back. "Don't worry. The detail's all there if they ask. But I think they'll appreciate us cutting to the chase. If anything, being able to explain complexity in simple terms makes us look more in command of the details, not less. It shows we understand it well enough to boil it down."

Jenna nodded in agreement. "Plus, in our most recent working group session, communication was one area we identified as a client pain point. Remember how Barnwell's CEO said he often felt lost in our reports? We're directly addressing that."

Before Martin could reply, the door opened and in came the Barnwell team. There was Cheryl, the CFO, accompanied by her team of accountants, and right behind them the CEO, Tom Barnwell himself, a tall man in his fifties with a warm handshake, joined by two regional store managers and the head of operations. It was a broader audience than usual for a financial review meeting, which made Alex all the more glad they had tailored the content for a non-financial crowd as well.

Pleasantries were exchanged and everyone settled. After introductions, Alex kicked off the presentation. "Thank you for making time today," he began. "We're here to walk through the key insights from 2025. We've structured today's discussion a bit differently. Our goal is to focus on what matters most to your business, in plain language, and using visuals that tell the story of the numbers. We'll save detailed figures for the appendix or specific questions, we want this to be about understanding and action."

He saw Tom, the CEO, give an approving nod. Good.

Jenna advanced to the first content slide, titled *Sales Trends: What's Driving Growth.* On it was a simple bar chart showing monthly sales across regions with vibrant color coding, accompanied by a one-sentence summary: Consistent growth in the north region offset slight declines in the south, leading to a net 5% annual increase. Below that, three bullet points highlighted factors like a successful summer promotion (with a small sun icon the AI had suggested adding for a visual cue), an uptick in online store sales, and the closure of two underperforming outlets in the south.

Cheryl, the CFO, leaned forward. "This is immediately clear," she said. "I remember last year's slide for this, about 3 times as many bars and a table of numbers. This... I can see the story at a glance."

Encouraged, Alex continued. He spoke about each point, providing a bit of context, but kept the language accessible. Martin chimed in to answer a detailed question from Cheryl about the specific numbers behind that 5% growth, referring to the appendix when needed. The conversation was flowing naturally, with the Barnwell team engaging more than Alex had ever seen.

They moved on to a slide about Customer Behavior Insights, which featured a simple illustration of a shopping cart next to a data point about increase in average basket size. Jenna had used an AI to create a friendly infographic depicting a shopper, which now sat on the slide. One of the store managers, seeing it, smiled and said, "I like that little graphic. It's silly, but it actually helped me remember the number you just said about basket size increasing 10%. I'll be able to tell my staff this and they'll get it."

As the presentation went on, Alex observed something remarkable: the CEO, Tom, was not glancing at his phone or whispering side comments to his operations head as he had in some past meetings. Instead, he was fully attentive, even leaning forward with interest. When they reached the cash flow slide that Jenna had been proud of, Tom actually raised his hand and interjected, "Hold on, this is the first time I think I really understand our cash flow position at a glance. This chart is excellent. So it looks like the main reason we had a dip in Q3 was the one-time warehouse investment, right? And otherwise, our operations are cash-positive?"

Alex confirmed, pleased to see Tom picking up the key insight. "Yes, exactly. The warehouse investment was a planned dip, and aside from that your operations are generating consistent cash. The chart shows the monthly net cash movement, green bars up are positive flows, red bar down in Q3 for that big investment, then back to green."

Tom nodded, smiling. "This visual makes it so clear. Honestly, in previous years I always had to ask Cheryl to interpret for me afterward. I appreciate how you've made this accessible."

Cheryl laughed, "He's not exaggerating, usually right after you folks leave, he'd stick his head in my office and say 'Alright, now in English, what did they say?'" The room shared a light chuckle.

One of the regional managers spoke up, gesturing to the slide on operating expenses that had a concise summary and a pie chart highlighting the biggest cost categories. "This might be the first finance meeting I've been in where I'm not overwhelmed by slides of tiny text. I can actually follow and see how this connects to what we experience in the stores. Thank you for that."

Martin shot a quick, relieved glance at Alex. Things were going even better than hoped.

They wrapped up the presentation with a slide titled Key Takeaways and Actions. Instead of dense paragraphs, it presented three callout boxes in plain language:

- Maintain momentum in North Region: Focus marketing where growth is strong.
- Address South Region declines: New strategy for underperforming stores in Q1.
- Leverage increased online sales: Invest in e-commerce and inventory integration.

Each was accompanied by a small icon (an upward arrow, a store, and a computer respectively) to reinforce the point. These bullet points were all generated with the help of AI suggestions in both wording and imagery.

Alex concluded, "We've included these key actions we recommend based on the data. In the full report, we detail some specific tactics under each, but at a high level, these are where we see opportunities for Barnwell Retail going into next year."

When the meeting opened for final questions, Tom cleared his throat. "I'll just say, this is the first time I've sat through one of these and fully grasped everything as we went. It's actually... exciting." He looked around at his team. "Usually these reviews are a chore, to be honest. But I feel like I have a clear picture of our business now. Alex, Jenna, Martin, great job. Please pass my thanks to anyone else back at your firm who worked on making this presentation so clear. I assume it took extra effort to simplify things so well."

Jenna smiled and answered, "It did take effort, but we also tried some new tools to help us refine the messaging. We learned that a little extra time spent on clarity can go a long way."

Cheryl added, "I agree with Tom. I think this sets a new bar for how we interpret our data. And likely it'll spark better conversations on our end as well."

With that, the formal meeting ended on a high note. As the Barnwell team departed or stayed to chat, Tom shook hands again with each of the presenters. "Looking forward to next quarter's review already if it's going to be like this," he said brightly.

After packing up, Alex and his team walked out to their cars in the crisp afternoon air. Martin let out a whoop once they were out of earshot of the building. "That was amazing! Did you hear them? I've never seen a client so pumped about a financial review."

Jenna laughed, "I know, right? It felt more like a strategy session than us just dumping numbers on them."

Alex was quiet, reflecting. "This is what it's all about," he finally said. "We spend so many hours analyzing and checking, but if the insight doesn't get across, it's like it never happened. Today we bridged that gap."

He unlocked the car and threw his bag in the back. "And we couldn't have done it as effectively without those AI tools helping us refine our communication, summarizing the data, polishing the language, even making the visuals friendlier."

Martin buckled into the passenger seat. "It's funny, I was worried using AI might make our work seem less personal or too automated. But it actually let us focus on the human part, the story, the understanding."

"Exactly," Alex agreed as he started the engine. He remembered how initial conversations about AI at the firm had revolved mostly around efficiency and cost-saving. Those were true, but this outcome felt different. It felt more meaningful. "I think this shows that AI's real value isn't just making our lives easier internally. It's helping us do better by our clients."

That evening, back at the office, Alex drafted a quick email to Marcus and Priya, who had been eager to hear how the Barnwell meeting went. He described the positive feedback and highlighted how the AI-assisted clarity had made a tangible difference. Within minutes, Priya responded with a confetti emoji and, "This is awesome! Let's share this success story in the next all-hands." Marcus's reply was simply, "Proud of the team. This is the future of client service, making things easier for them, not just for us."

Alex smiled at the responses and shut down his laptop for the night. As he walked out to his car once more to head home, he thought about how far they'd come from the days when dense binders of reports were the norm. This new approach felt right.

Today confirmed it: when we use AI to make our work clearer and more human-friendly, everyone wins. Efficiency is great, but helping a client truly understand and succeed, that's the real success. With AI's help, we're not just working faster; we're serving better.

Chapter 18: AI at Home, Everyday Wins

Late Saturday morning, sunlight filtered through the kitchen window as Maria carefully packed a finished batch of lavender-scented candles into boxes. The kitchen counter had been transformed into her small business workshop, filled with drying candles, labels, and packing material. She wiped her brow with the back of her hand, leaving a tiny streak of gold wax on her skin. Business was good, better than she had expected when she started this candle-making venture six months ago, and in no small part due to a secret helper: the AI tools she'd adopted to handle tasks beyond her crafting talent.

With the candles safely boxed, Maria opened her laptop at the dining table, where a half-eaten piece of toast and a mug of tea sat amidst her notes. First on her to-do list: creating a social media post to announce her new "Autumn Glow" candle collection. In the past, this would have taken her hours of agonizing over phrasing and maybe a nudge from Alex. But now she had another source of inspiration.

She typed a prompt into her AI assistant: *"Help me write a warm, engaging Instagram post introducing a new candle scent for fall, called Autumn Glow. Mention the scent notes (pumpkin, cinnamon, vanilla) and add a touch of storytelling about cozy evenings."* The cursor blinked for a second, then a draft began to appear. Maria watched as the sentences formed: *"As the nights get cooler, light an Autumn Glow candle and let the pumpkin, cinnamon, and vanilla notes wrap you in a cozy hug. I created this scent thinking of my family's fall evenings, warm blankets, good books, and the comfort of home. #AutumnGlow #Handmade"*

Maria smiled. "That's a lovely start," she murmured. She tweaked a few words to better match her own voice, but the bulk of the creative heavy lifting was done. With a few clicks, she scheduled the post to go live in the afternoon.

As she closed the app, Maria reflected on how far she'd come. Just a few months ago, she remembered staring at a blank screen, struggling to find the right words for her very first product description. Alex had cautiously suggested trying an AI writing tool back then. At first, Maria hesitated, it felt strange, almost like cheating at creativity. But when she finally gave it a shot, the AI helped turn her raw thoughts into a warm, polished paragraph. It still sounded like *her*, just a version with the umms and ahhs refined. That small win gave her the confidence to experiment more. Bit by bit, these tools had become like a trusted assistant, helping her shine in areas she used to dread. And customers responded, every thoughtfully written post and pretty label seemed to bring a small uptick in website visits or a new face discovering her candles.

Next, she turned to label design. Spread out on the table were some initial sketches she had drawn for the Autumn Glow label, a simple outline of a fall leaf and a small pumpkin icon. Drawing wasn't her strong suit, so earlier in the week she had tried something new: using an AI image generator to refine her concept. She opened the design file now, recalling how amazed she'd been. By describing her idea ("a minimalist label with a single autumn leaf and a small pumpkin icon, in warm orange tones"), the AI had provided several polished variations. She ended up selecting one, tweaking the colors slightly, and adding her brand name in a charming, AI-suggested font that evoked autumn. The result was sitting right in front of her, a professionally styled label that she felt proud to stick onto each candle jar.

Maria began affixing the new labels to the jars for the next batch. As she did, her phone chimed with a new email notification. A customer from out of state had sent a message inquiring about international shipping options, something Maria hadn't dealt with before. She bit her lip, wondering how to respond professionally and helpfully. Then she remembered: she didn't have to draft it alone. Grabbing her laptop again, Maria opened ChatGPT and wrote: *"Draft a polite, friendly email responding to a customer inquiry about international shipping for my candle business. Mention I'm a small business owner and I will look into options."*

Within moments, the AI offered a draft: *"Hello there! Thank you so much for your interest in my candles and for reaching out. I'm a small business owner based in Texas, and I'm thrilled you'd like to enjoy my products across borders. I currently ship within the U.S., but I'm actively exploring international shipping options. I'll do some research on the best way to get an Autumn Glow candle to you, and I'll update you within the next few days. Thank you for your patience and support! Warm regards, Maria."*

Maria read it over and nodded. It was gracious and clear. She added a personal P.S. about how she'd love to share a bit of Texas autumn with the customer and then hit send. What might have taken her a half hour of fretting over wording was now done in a few minutes, and with confidence that it struck the right tone.

With those tasks done, Maria turned to one last item she'd been procrastinating on: writing a short "Founder's Note" for her website. She wanted to tell the story of how she started this candle business, to give it a personal touch. She'd scribbled bullet points in her notebook, childhood memories of making candles with her grandmother, the joy of creating scents that made people feel at home, the decision to finally turn a hobby into something more. But writing it out eloquently was daunting.

She took a breath, opened a blank document, and started writing in her own words. After a few sentences, she hesitated, unsure if the tone was right. So she tried a different approach. "Let's do this together," she thought, and wrote a new prompt to the AI: *"Help me write a short, heartfelt founder's story for my candle business. Include why I started, what I love about it, and thank the customers."* The AI responded with a beautifully structured piece. Maria didn't copy it wholesale, that wouldn't feel authentic, but it gave her a structure and some phrases that resonated. She merged it with her own drafts, spent some time tweaking and infusing more of her personal anecdotes, and soon she had a Founder's Note that truly reflected her voice, only clearer.

By early afternoon, Maria's tasks were done. The Instagram post was already getting likes and comments ("This sounds amazing, can't wait to try!" one user wrote). Her website now had a heartfelt story that she felt did justice to her passion. And her inbox had a grateful reply from the overseas customer, who appreciated her looking into shipping and said they'd wait eagerly for her update. Maria felt a wave of accomplishment and relief. Running a small business was still hard work, but with a bit of AI help, she was able to manage areas that had been weaknesses and turn them into strengths. It felt like she had a capable (if invisible) assistant by her side, letting her focus more on the creative and personal parts she loved most.

That evening, the aroma of tomato sauce and baked cheese filled the dining room as the family sat down to dinner. Alex had declared it homemade-pizza night, partly as an excuse to celebrate a week of victories big and small. At the table were Alex, Maria, and Sophie, who was eagerly loading her plate with a second slice.

"I have to say," Alex grinned, raising his slice in a mock toast, "to Maria, for officially becoming an international businesswoman!"

Maria laughed. "Hardly," she said, "I haven't even figured out the shipping part yet."

"But you will, Mom," Sophie chimed in confidently. "Your candles are awesome. Everyone in my school who got one from us as a holiday gift last year still talks about them."

Maria reached over to squeeze Sophie's hand. "Thank you, sweetie. Actually, I might need your help with something techy later, maybe figuring out the shipping rates website. I'm sure you'll navigate it faster than me."

"Deal," Sophie said, before adding playfully, "for a small consulting fee, of course."

Alex almost spat out his drink laughing. "Consulting fee, huh? That's my girl, already learning the value of her services!"

Sophie giggled and took a sip of her water. "Speaking of school... I got the results of my project today." Her eyes sparkled with pride.

"Oh! The one on AI, right?" Maria prompted. "We've been so busy today I forgot to ask how it went. Tell us!"

Sophie straightened up, putting on a modestly serious face that mimicked a news reporter. "I am pleased to report that I got an A-plus, and Mr. Diaz said my presentation was 'exceptionally thoughtful'." She couldn't hold the proud smile back any longer.

"That's amazing!" Alex exclaimed. "Congratulations!" He and Maria both reached to give Sophie a hug, nearly causing her to drop her pizza.

Sophie laughed and waved them off lightly. "Okay, okay! You want to hear about it or not?"

"Of course, we do," Maria said, dabbing her lips with a napkin and giving full attention.

Sophie described how her class had been assigned to present on a technology topic of their choice. Many of her classmates did flashy demonstrations, one boy showed off a game mod he made with AI, another girl had an AI draw pictures based on classmate suggestions in real time. Those were cool, but Sophie took a different angle. "I titled mine 'AI: A Helpful Friend, With Good Manners'," she said. "I talked about how we can use AI in our daily lives, but also about being responsible. I even mentioned how Dad's company has guidelines and how you guys always remind me to check if information is true, not to just copy-paste things, and stuff like that."

Alex raised an eyebrow. "You quoted our dinner table lectures, did you?"

"Maybe a little," Sophie smirked. "I gave examples too. Like how I used that history chatbot to get ideas for my history essay last month but then verified the facts in the textbook.

And how Mom uses design AI but still adds her own touch. Mr. Diaz said he loved that I talked about ethics and creativity, not just the cool factor. I think that's why I got the extra credit for creativity and critical thinking."

Maria reached for a slice of garlic bread, looking impressed. "Sophie, that's wonderful. It sounds like you taught the class something important. I'm proud that you understand technology is a tool, and it's up to us to use it thoughtfully."

Sophie shrugged happily. "Well, I had good teachers here at home."

Alex felt his heart swell a little at that. This was one of those moments a parent lives for, seeing your child internalize values you hoped to impart. "You know," he said, "this really has turned into a year of learning for all of us. And here we are, each of us finding ways to succeed with a little help from AI."

He raised his glass of sparkling water. "To adaptation and progress," he declared.

Maria and Sophie raised theirs to clink. "Adaptation and progress," they echoed, the glasses chiming softly.

As they sipped and dug back into dinner, the conversation turned to lighthearted plans for the weekend, Sophie lobbying for a camping trip, Maria joking that only if they could bring an AI to set up the tent, laughter all around.

Later that night, with the house quiet and everyone else asleep, Alex sat in his study flipping through the pages of his notebook. He found a fresh page and uncapped his pen. There was a thought crystallizing in his mind, something he wanted to capture in ink, a simple truth that had become clear through all these experiences at work and at home.

He began to write, the pen scratching softly in the silence.

> We embraced change, and it changed us, for the better.
>
> Adaptation isn't about keeping up, it's about growing stronger together.
>
> AI didn't replace our human touch; it enriched it.
>
> This is how we move forward, hand in hand with progress.

Chapter 19: Moving Forward, Together

Alex stepped into the packed conference room with a mix of excitement and calm confidence. This day had been circled on his calendar for weeks, the day the company would formally adopt the updated AI guidelines. As he looked around the long table, he saw colleagues from every department present, including Robert, who offered a reassuring nod. The atmosphere buzzed with anticipation.

The CTO cleared her throat and addressed the room. "Thank you all for being here. Today marks an important milestone for us." She smiled at Alex and the rest of the AI working group seated near him. "Over the past few months, Alex and his team have worked tirelessly to refine our AI usage guidelines. I'm pleased to announce that leadership has reviewed and *unanimously approved* the new AI Guidelines, including Robert's reconciliation workflow." A round of polite applause filled the room, swelling into genuine enthusiasm as the news sank in.

Alex felt a warm flush of pride. He exchanged a glance with Robert, recalling how just a short while ago they were on opposite sides of a debate. Robert had been skeptical about relying on AI for certain sensitive tasks, worried about errors slipping through. In response, he developed a step-by-step *reconciliation workflow* to ensure that any AI-generated output was double-checked and validated by a human expert before final decisions were made. By bridging the gap between AI efficiency and human oversight, Robert's idea had strengthened the guidelines, and the trust between colleagues. Now it was officially part of company policy. Robert gave Alex a thumbs-up from across the table, and Alex returned the gesture with a grateful smile.

As the meeting continued, department heads discussed how they would implement the guidelines in their teams. The conversation was lively but positive, *a far cry from the uncertainty and hesitation* that had filled similar meetings at the beginning of Alex's journey. Marketing talked about using the guidelines to vet AI-generated campaign ideas, Finance planned to integrate them into their risk analysis AI tools, and HR even mentioned developing training around ethical AI use for new hires. Alex took careful notes, ready to follow up and offer support. This was exactly what he had hoped for: people not just accepting the change, but actively *engaging* with it.

When the formal discussion wrapped up, Mr. Morales stood to say a few words. "I want to acknowledge the exceptional initiative Alex has shown," he began, looking directly at him. Alex's face warmed as all eyes turned his way. "Leading the AI working group, rallying colleagues from different departments, and staying committed to responsible innovation, this is the kind of leadership that moves us forward." Alex felt a swell of emotion: gratitude, pride, and a touch of disbelief. The CEO continued, "In fact, our company has been invited to speak on an industry panel about AI adoption next month, and we'd like Alex to represent us and share our story."

Surprise flickered through Alex's mind, followed by excitement. A few colleagues broke into spontaneous applause, and the CTO clapped him on the back. Alex managed to find his voice. "Thank you. I'm honored... and, well, this wouldn't have been possible without everyone in this room." He gestured to his team and the other leaders, wanting them to share in the credit. "Our journey was a group effort."

After the meeting, people lingered to chat. Several department heads came up to Alex to express their appreciation and to ask when his AI Committee would start the promised lunch-and-learn sessions. "We're eager to learn how to apply these guidelines in our daily work," said one manager from Operations. Alex grinned, energized by their eagerness. "Our first session is next week," he replied. "We'll be covering practical tips on using AI tools responsibly. And don't worry, there will be plenty of time for Q&A, feel free to bring your lunch and your questions." Word had already spread that Alex's committee planned to host informal *Lunch-and-Learn* workshops to help colleagues make sense of the new guidelines. What started as a small passion project now had a company-wide audience.

Robert joined Alex as he packed up his notes. "Not bad for a skeptic, huh?" Robert quipped, referring to himself. "Your reconciliation workflow was the missing piece we needed," Alex said sincerely. They walked out together, reflecting on how much had changed. A few months ago, Alex had been apprehensive about even suggesting an AI committee; now he was helping lead the entire company through an AI-driven transformation. Robert, once unsure about AI's reliability, had become one of its cleverest advocates by finding a way to make human expertise and AI work hand-in-hand. They both had grown, and so had the company culture around them.

That evening, Alex returned home tired but happy. The aroma of garlic and tomatoes greeted him as he stepped into the kitchen. Maria was at the stove, stirring a pot of her signature pasta sauce. Sophie sat at the table, textbooks and her tablet spread out in front of her. It was a cozy, familiar scene that always grounded him no matter how hectic his day had been.

Maria turned and immediately noticed the spring in Alex's step. "From the smile on your face, I take it the big meeting went well?" she asked, arching an eyebrow playfully. Alex laughed and moved to give her a warm hug, mindful of the wooden spoon in her hand. "It did. They approved all of our AI guidelines, officially. And..." he drew back to look at her, still a bit in awe, "they want me to speak at an industry panel next month."

Maria's eyes lit up. "Alex, that's amazing! I'm so proud of you." Sophie looked up from her tablet, having caught the last part. "A panel? Like, in front of a lot of people?" she asked. There was both curiosity and admiration in her tone. Alex nodded and ruffled her hair gently as he passed by to wash his hands. "Yes, in front of a lot of people. I'll be talking about how our company adopted AI responsibly. Honestly, I'm a little nervous."

"You'll do great, Dad," Sophie said confidently. "You've basically been doing that at home with us and at work already." Maria nodded in agreement. "Exactly. Remember how you walked me through using that new AI scheduling tool for my business? You have a talent for explaining things in a way that clicks."

Alex smiled, his heart warm. "Thanks. I guess practice at home helped me find the right words for work too." He set the table as they talked. "Speaking of your business," he added, "how are things going with your new AI helper?"

Maria's face brightened. She set the spoon down and turned to lean against the counter, her eyes shining with excitement. "Honestly, it's been a game changer. I feel so much more confident running everything now." She began ticking off on her fingers. "Inventory management? The AI keeps track and reminds me to restock before I even notice things running low. Customer inquiries? The chatbot on our website answers most common questions instantly, even at 2 AM, and it does it in a friendly way that sounds like me. And marketing... well, you remember how lost I felt trying to come up with social media posts." Alex recalled the evenings Maria had spent staring at a blank screen, stressing over the perfect words to promote her handmade crafts. Maria continued, "Now I draft a few ideas with the AI's help and then tweak them to add my personal touch. What used to take me hours now takes maybe 30 minutes, and I actually enjoy it."

"That's wonderful, honey," Alex said, meaning it. He remembered how skeptical Maria had been at first, understandably so. She had built her small online business from scratch and was protective of every part of it. The idea of handing off tasks to an AI assistant had made her uneasy, as if she were cheating or might lose control. They had many late-night chats about it, and Alex had shared what he was learning: that using AI isn't about replacing the human touch, but enhancing it. Seeing Maria now, clearly more at ease and confident, filled him with pride. She had grown just as he had.

Sophie interjected with a dramatic sigh, pushing aside one of her textbooks. "I wish some of my classmates would realize AI is for helping, not doing everything for you." At this, Alex and Maria exchanged a knowing glance. Sophie had been navigating her own journey with AI at school, and not without bumps. Alex gently probed, "Something on your mind?"

Sophie nodded, her expression a mix of frustration and determination. "We had a history essay last week, and the teacher ran it through a plagiarism checker. Some kids just copied AI-written content verbatim. They got caught, obviously, and now the principal is concerned we're all misusing AI." She rolled her eyes. "But some of us actually used it the right way! I had the AI help me brainstorm ideas and find sources, but I wrote the essay myself and cited everything. I even showed my drafts to prove it."

Maria placed a comforting hand on Sophie's shoulder. "And I'm sure your teacher recognized that." Sophie brightened a little. "Yeah, Mr. Diaz did. In fact..." She sat up straighter, a hint of pride creeping into her voice. "He asked me and a couple of other students to help co-design a student workshop on responsible AI use. They want us to share our experiences and maybe come up with guidelines for students, like a 'smart AI use' honor code or something."

"Wow, Sophie, that's terrific," Alex said. He felt a surge of pride, similar to what he felt when the CEO praised his work, perhaps even stronger. "You're turning into a leader yourself, you know that?" Sophie blushed and shrugged, trying to play it cool. "I just... I just want people my age to get it. AI's not going away, so we need to learn how to use it without turning into robots or, you know, breaking the rules."

Alex chuckled. "Spoken like a true *Adaptive Professional*-in-training." Sophie giggled at the title. Maria laughed too, "Maybe she'll write her own book someday."

They sat down to dinner, the conversation flowing easily from Sophie's upcoming science fair to the plans for Alex's panel presentation. It struck Alex how *normal* this all felt now. A few months ago, AI was an almost constant source of anxiety under their roof, whether it was his own job worries, Maria's hesitations, or concerns about Sophie's schoolwork. Now AI had become a helpful, well-integrated part of their lives. It didn't dominate the conversation with fear or uncertainty; it was just another interesting topic, one of many ways they were all growing and doing new things.

After dinner, the family migrated to the living room. While Sophie headed off to draft some ideas for the school workshop ("I'll show you my slides later, Dad," she promised), Alex and Maria curled up on the couch with cups of tea. The house was quiet, save for the gentle tapping of Sophie's keyboard in the next room. Alex felt a deep contentment settle over him.

He thought back to the early days of this journey. In his mind's eye, he saw a version of himself hunched over a notebook late at night, scribbling worries like "Will AI make my skills obsolete?" and "How do I keep up?" He remembered the weight of uncertainty, the nights he'd lain awake imagining the worst, that he'd be left behind in his career, unable to provide for his family, or that he wouldn't understand the new tools well enough and he'd make a disastrous mistake at work. Those fears had driven him to take action, to learn and adapt.

Looking at where he stood now, Alex almost wanted to chuckle at his past self. Not out of ridicule, but out of relief and understanding. Yes, it had been hard at first. Adapting required humility, admitting what he didn't know, and courage to face the unknown. It required patience, collaboration, and a willingness to fail and try again. But every step had been worth it. AI, which he once viewed as a threat or a challenge to overcome, had become a partner. By leaning into learning, Alex found that AI actually amplified his human abilities: it took over the drudge work and freed him to be more creative and strategic. It flagged problems he might have missed and offered solutions he hadn't considered, essentially acting like a teammate who was tireless and knowledgeable. With AI's support, Alex had more time to mentor his colleagues, to think big-picture, and even to spend precious evenings helping Sophie with her homework or brainstorming with Maria.

And it wasn't just him. Watching Maria and Sophie adapt in their own ways was perhaps the most fulfilling part. He had always wanted to set a good example for his daughter; now Sophie was blossoming into a responsible young tech user who might influence her peers for the better. Maria, too, had gained a new sense of confidence and balance, juggling her business with family life more smoothly.

Alex finished his tea and set the cup down on the coffee table. Maria had dozed off against his shoulder, the long day catching up with her. Gently, so as not to wake her, Alex slipped away and stood up. He felt a familiar pull, a small voice in his mind suggesting he capture this moment, this feeling, while it was fresh. It was the same urge that had made him start jotting in his notebook months ago when this adventure began.

He stepped quietly into his study and switched on the desk lamp. The old leather-bound notebook lay on the desk, its pages filled with the story of his transformation in scrawled notes, ideas, and reflections. Alex ran his fingers over the cover, then opened to the next blank page. He thought about everything that had led to this moment, the challenges, the skepticism, the breakthroughs and the hard-won lessons. How could he sum it up? He wanted to write something for himself, to crystallize what he'd learned, but also something that might speak to anyone out there who was like he had been: anxious about the future, unsure of how to take that first step to adapt.

Alex picked up his pen, the faint scratch of the nib on paper the only sound in the night. In clear, bold letters he began to write his final entry in the notebook.

> Evolving with AI taught me that the future isn't something that just happens to me; it's something I can help shape.
>
> AI didn't replace my value, it revealed how I could add more.
>
> We grow best when we adapt hand-in-hand with our tools and one another.
>
> This is how we move forward, together.

Epilogue

Alex stood backstage in the hushed semi-darkness, fingertips resting on the smooth pages of his well-worn notebook. Beyond the heavy curtain he could hear the low murmur of an audience settling into their seats. The conference hall was filled with hundreds, perhaps over a thousand, of professionals waiting to hear him speak. A faint tremor of nerves ran through him, but it was a different kind of nervousness than a year ago. This was anticipation, not anxiety. He drew in a slow breath, straightened his posture, and allowed himself a small, proud smile. One year ago, he could never have imagined himself here.

The neon sign outside had his name emblazoned alongside the words *Keynote Speaker*. It still felt surreal. Alex Harper, once the hesitant manager who'd quietly experimented with AI tools in the shadows of his office, was now a respected voice on integrating AI in the workplace. He gently tapped his trusty notebook with the end of his favorite pen, a small ritual that kept him grounded. That notebook had seen him through a year of transformation, evolving from a place where he once scribbled tentative ideas into a personal journal of lessons learned. Even as everything around him went digital, he still found comfort in those analog pages.

A polite knock on the backstage door interrupted his thoughts. It was one of the event coordinators peeking in to give him a ten-minute warning. Alex smiled and thanked her. As the door clicked shut, he exhaled and assured himself that he *was* ready. In the front row out there sat industry leaders, curious skeptics, and old-school experts, people who a year ago might have been him. Now they were here to listen to how an ordinary professional had adapted and thrived.

He closed his notebook and set aside his scripted notes. He had rehearsed thoroughly, but planned to speak from the heart, sharing stories of the people who took this journey with him. Those people were on his mind now. Alex reached for his phone to check the flurry of messages that had buzzed in throughout the morning. He typically silenced his phone before a talk, but today he felt he needed to see these. The screen lit up with words of encouragement from friends and colleagues, each a reminder of why he was here.

The first message he opened was from Maria. In it she was beaming in a selfie, holding up one of her handcrafted candles. *"Good luck today!"* her text read, followed by, *"Remember, you helped light the way for me, now go inspire some more folks!"* She added proudly that her candle business had just surpassed a quarter-million dollars in sales, thanks to a bit of "digital magic" they'd implemented. Alex chuckled warmly. Trust Maria to weave a candle metaphor into a pep talk.

He took a moment to reflect on how far Maria had come. A year ago, her artisan candle venture was a humble side gig in her garage. She'd been struggling to keep up, hand-pouring candles by night and juggling customer emails and shipping by day. Alex vividly remembered sitting with her late one evening amid towers of shipping boxes and half-melted wax, walking her through the basics of an AI chatbot to answer customer questions and an automated system to handle her online marketing. Technology wasn't Maria's first language, but that night she embraced it out of sheer necessity and hope.

In the months that followed, Maria turned those tools into her silent business partners. Routine questions from customers were handled by her "AI assistant" while she focused on crafting new scents. With less time spent on administrative chores, she managed to scale up rapidly. Now her candles were featured in boutique shops across the country, and she even hosted workshops to mentor other artisans about blending traditional crafts with digital tools. Embracing AI hadn't changed Maria's mission, it had amplified her voice, letting her share her craft with a far wider audience. Alex felt a swell of pride reading her message, knowing he'd played a small part in her journey.

Next, Alex opened a message from Sophie. She'd sent a short video clip of her high school classroom where she stood at the front, leading a discussion for her "AI Ethics & Creativity Club." In the video, Sophie's voice was clear and passionate as she engaged her classmates on how AI could help environmental science. The caption she added made him smile: *"They actually listened to me, Dad! Wish you could've been here."*

It was hard for Alex to believe how much Sophie had grown into a leader in just a year. He remembered a dinner table debate not long ago, when she had challenged him about relying too much on AI. She had worried about creativity and ethics, pushing him to consider perspectives he hadn't thought of. That conversation spurred Sophie to start the AI Ethics club at school, determined that her generation approach technology thoughtfully.

Now 17 and in her senior year of high school, Sophie had been accepted to a top university. She planned to study environmental science and use AI to tackle real-world problems like climate change. Her blend of caution and optimism toward technology gave Alex so much hope. Watching that video, seeing her confidently moderate a discussion, he felt as proud as ever. In his talk, he'd be mentioning Sophie's story as proof that the next generation isn't just ready to use AI, they're ready to guide it responsibly. The future, he thought, was in very good hands.

Glancing out through the curtain, Alex spotted Robert in the front row. Robert flashed him an encouraging wave, and Alex felt a rush of gratitude. Robert had been his closest colleague at work in the journey to bring AI into their firm. Early on, Robert was the quiet analyst who took notice when Alex first experimented with an AI tool to summarize a meeting. Intrigued, Robert tried it himself and was amazed at the efficiency. Together, they cautiously introduced their small success to the rest of the team.

What began as two coworkers testing a new idea soon became a company-wide shift in workflow. Within months, and with management's blessing, Alex and Robert helped implement AI-assisted processes across multiple departments. Robert truly found his stride in that process. The once-reserved numbers guy grew into an in-house evangelist for smart automation. He started hosting workshops to teach colleagues how to use AI in their daily tasks and personally coached every new hire on "AI literacy." The transformation was remarkable: Robert evolved from working quietly behind spreadsheets to confidently standing in front of conference rooms, guiding others.

Seeing him here now, notebook in hand and a proud grin on his face, Alex felt a deep kinship. They had pushed each other to be bolder. Robert's journey was living proof that with a bit of courage and collaboration, even a traditional workplace could turn innovation into the new normal. His presence in the audience steadied Alex's nerves, a reminder that he wasn't going into this alone, but carrying the strength of their shared experience with him.

Just then, Alex's phone buzzed again, this time with a notification from the company's social media feed. Priya had just tagged him in a post. The image she shared made him grin: a cute cartoon of a nervous figure at the bottom of a staircase and a confident figure at the top behind a podium, clearly depicting Alex's journey from beginner to keynote speaker. Her caption read: *"From newbie to keynote in one year! Give 'em your best, Alex. You got this!"*

Priya's own growth in the past year had been extraordinary. When Alex first met her, she was the quiet junior accountant who rarely strayed beyond her spreadsheets. She wasn't sure how AI could possibly help in accounting, a world of rules and numbers. But one day she got a taste of AI's creative side. She saw colleagues using a custom AI model to brainstorm marketing ideas, and it intrigued her. Alex had encouraged her to give those tools a try. To everyone's surprise, including her own, Priya discovered a flair for creative work. She began experimenting with an AI writing assistant to draft fun internal memos and used an image generator to spice up presentations.

Before long, she had taken on a dual role: balancing the books by morning and managing the company's social media by afternoon. She even trained her ChatGPT on the company's tone to help craft posts, which she then refined with her personal touch. Freed from her self-imposed limits, she blossomed. Her social media campaigns boosted the company's engagement significantly. She often joked that playing with AI let her "color outside the lines" and made her day job more rewarding.

Alex shook his head in amazement at the memory. Priya's story was a perfect example of hidden talents unlocked by a willingness to try something new. He knew he'd be sharing her journey with the audience as a reminder that adaptability can spark personal growth in the most unexpected ways.

Finally, Alex opened a simple text from Mark that had arrived moments ago. *"Watching your talk live with my team. We're all rooting for you! That AI workflow template you shared is now the backbone of our planning here. I wouldn't be here without your help. Now go knock 'em dead out there!"*

Alex felt his throat tighten with emotion. Mark's journey was perhaps the most dramatic of them all. A year ago, he had been unemployed, sitting across from Alex at their favorite coffee shop, worn down and uncertain. Decades of steady work had ended abruptly, and he was struggling to make sense of what came next. His résumé felt outdated, his confidence even more so. Together, they spent hours reworking his materials, drafting new cover letters, and role-playing interview questions. Alex encouraged him to highlight what machines could never replace: his experience, his reliability, and his instinct for solving problems.

Those efforts paid off. Within weeks, Mark landed a position at a regional logistics firm willing to take a chance on him because he showed a genuine curiosity about learning AI-based tools for route planning and inventory optimization. The first few months were tough, Mark often called Alex in the evenings, frustrated by how different everything felt. But he kept at it, building skill by skill, prompt by prompt, until things began to click. Before long, he wasn't just keeping up, he was innovating.

Now, a year later, Mark had become one of the firm's most valuable employees. He used AI models to predict shipment delays and redesign delivery routes, cutting costs and improving efficiency. His reports were so accurate that upper management began relying on them to make key scheduling decisions. Around the office, people jokingly called him "the AI whisperer," and he had embraced the nickname with a laugh. True to form, he started helping others on his team, showing younger colleagues how to use the same tools that once intimidated him.

By mentoring others, Mark found renewed purpose. His transformation had gone far beyond employment, it was personal. The man who once felt obsolete now felt essential again, proof that curiosity and effort could rewrite anyone's story. Reading Mark's message that morning, Alex felt a swell of pride. Mark's success was more than a comeback; it was a reminder of why Alex believed so deeply in this work, to make sure that no one, regardless of age or background, was left behind in this new era of change.

He hadn't expected any more surprises, but just then a familiar voice spoke softly behind him. "Ready, Alex?"

He turned to see Blaze standing at the edge of the curtain, half illuminated by the glow of the stage lights. Alex's face broke into a grin. "Blaze! You made it?"

Blaze stepped forward with his trademark easy smile. "Of course I did. Not too long ago you were in my bootcamp class, and now look at you, about to go on stage as the expert. I wouldn't miss this for the world." He gave Alex a quick, encouraging pat on the arm.

Alex felt a surge of gratitude. Blaze's AI bootcamp had been the spark that started it all, giving him the knowledge and confidence to push forward. "I'm glad you're here," Alex said earnestly. "I don't think I'd be here without your help back then."

"Hey, you did the work. I just pointed you in the right direction," Blaze replied, his eyes shining with pride. "Just be yourself out there. Speak from the heart, like you always do. They're going to love it."

Alex nodded, absorbing the pep talk. "Will do." He took one last deep breath, feeling his nerves settle into steady determination.

Blaze squeezed his shoulder. "Go get 'em, Alex." With that, Blaze slipped back into the shadows of the wing, leaving Alex alone with the stage just a few steps away.

On cue, the muffled voice of the emcee began announcing Alex's name and accomplishments to the audience. This was it. Alex stepped up to the edge of the curtain, notebook still in hand. Before walking out, he flipped to a blank page. In a spontaneous moment of reflection, he put pen to paper and jotted down a final thought. It was a brief message to himself, one that captured everything he'd learned in this remarkable year.

> One year ago I was hesitant about the future. Today, I'm about to address a crowd on how to embrace it. We've learned that adapting isn't about becoming someone else, it's about becoming the best version of ourselves, with a little help from new tools.
>
> I once feared being left behind; now I know that no one gets left behind if we help each other along. If I can grow this much in a year, imagine what *you* can do.
>
> The journey doesn't end here, this is just the beginning.

Appendices: Putting It All Together

By this point in *The Adaptive Professional*, you have seen what it means to evolve. To stay curious, to reimagine your role, and to view change not as a threat but as an opportunity to grow. But reading about adaptability and living it are two different things.

These appendices are extensions of the book's purpose. Each one is designed to help you move from awareness to application, turning insight into practice and reflection into forward motion.

Think of them as your starter toolkit for continuous reinvention: simple, structured tools that will help you keep learning, experimenting, and growing long after you finish the story.

Here is what you will find:

Appendix A: Lessons Learned

A concise summary of the key takeaways from *The Adaptive Professional.*
This section distills the patterns that appeared throughout the book: what worked, what did not, and how professionals who adapt well think differently. Use it as a reference whenever you want to reconnect with the mindset of growth and resilience.

Appendix B: Quick Start Guide: How to Talk to ChatGPT for the First Time

For many readers, AI can feel abstract or overwhelming. This guide demystifies that first step by showing exactly how to begin a productive conversation with ChatGPT. You will see real examples of weak versus strong prompts, learn how to give AI context, and even find a script for when you do not know what to ask.

It is not about mastering technology. It is about mastering communication with it.

Appendix C: Productive Prompts for Reinvention and Renewal

Once you understand how to engage AI effectively, this section helps you apply it to real life. These ten prompt categories address the most common crossroads mid-career professionals face, from burnout to leadership transitions to career reinvention.

Each one provides ready-to-use language for reflection, planning, and growth. You can use them directly in ChatGPT or as personal journaling prompts to guide self-discovery.

Together, these three appendices give you the mindset, the method, and the means to continue adapting, not just once but throughout your career.

The world will keep changing. Tools will keep evolving. But adaptability is not about chasing every new thing. It is about staying open, intentional, and self-aware.

These final pages are here to help you do exactly that.

Appendix D: Adaptive Action Plan

This simple guide will help you apply what you've learned and grow with AI at your own pace. Use it to spot opportunities, try small experiments, and build confidence as you develop your own adaptive path forward.

Appendix A: Lessons Learned

Alex's journey began with hesitation and uncertainty, and ended with confidence, clarity, and a practical understanding of how to use AI as a trusted partner. These are the key lessons he noted along the way, part philosophy, part practice, for anyone learning to adapt in a changing world.

1. Adaptation Is a Choice

Fear fades when replaced by curiosity.
Start small, learn one tool, and build from there.
You don't need to master everything, only to begin.

The future doesn't wait for perfection, it rewards participation.

2. Learn Before You Leverage

Understand the basics: what AI is, how it works, and what it isn't.
AI (Artificial Intelligence) recognizes patterns and generates responses.
Machine Learning (ML) improves systems through data.
Large Language Models (LLMs), like ChatGPT, process and generate human-like text.

Learn the language of progress. It makes every new tool less intimidating.
When in doubt, ask: *"What does this tool actually do, and how can it help me think better?"*

3. Build Your Toolkit

These are the categories Alex mastered, examples will change, but the functions endure:

Category	Use Case	Example Tools
Writing & Ideas	Letters, resumes, brainstorming, summaries, rewriting,	ChatGPT, Claude, Gemini, Copilot, other AI assistants or chatbots
Visual Design	Images, graphics, layouts	Midjourney, Canva, DALL·E
Video & Avatars	Narration, explainers, talking avatars	HeyGen, Synthesia, D-ID
Organization	Notes, planning, automation	Notion AI, ClickUp, Otter.ai
Coding & Data	Code generation, scripts, spreadsheet analysis	ChatGPT Code Interpreter, Python
Marketing & Communication	Social posts, emails, outreach, content creation	Jasper, Copy.ai, Canva Magic Write

Tools, products, and companies will evolve, but the categories remain. Learn the concept, not the brand.

Appendix B: Quick Start Guide

How to Talk to ChatGPT for the First Time

(For readers who are just starting to explore AI)

First off, most AI's have free versions for anyone to use. Simple and free means you can try for no risk! If you've never used ChatGPT or another AI assistant before, here's the most important lesson:

AI can't read your mind, it responds to your clarity.

Think of it like a conversation with a sharp but uninformed intern. The more you explain who you are and what you want, the smarter its answers become.

Prompting: weak vs. strong

❌ Weak Prompt (Vague and Generic)

"I need a new job. What should I do?"

AI Response:
You might consider updating your résumé, networking, or exploring new opportunities online.

(Accurate, but not useful — it doesn't know you.)

✅ Strong Prompt (Context + Goal + Direction)

"I'm a 42-year-old project manager in the healthcare industry with 15 years of experience. I'm feeling ready for a change but want to stay in a field where my management and communication skills still matter. Can you suggest three realistic career transitions I could explore, and describe what new skills I'd need to make each one successful?"

AI Response (condensed):

1. **Healthcare Technology Implementation Manager** – builds on project and process skills while adding digital health and analytics.

2. **Corporate Training & Development Lead** – uses communication and leadership strengths; learn instructional design.

3. **Operations Consultant for Healthcare Startups** – applies your experience in fast-moving organizations; add financial modeling and strategy.

(Much more relevant because you gave the AI the right information to adapt to you.)

3 Quick Tips to Get Great Results

1. Start with who you are.
Give a short bio: your role, experience, and what you're working on.

2. State your goal clearly.
Tell the AI what outcome you want (ideas, plan, explanation, etc.).

3. Iterate.
Treat it like a dialogue. Ask, *"Can you make that more actionable?"* or *"Show me examples."*

Example Prompt for Readers to Try

"I'm a mid-career professional working in [industry] with about [X] years of experience.
My biggest challenge right now is [describe briefly].

I want to use AI to help me [goal].
What are three ways I could get started today?"

If You Don't Know What to Ask

It's completely normal to open ChatGPT and freeze, unsure where to begin. You don't have to start with a perfect question. Start with curiosity. Tell the AI you're new, describe where you are in life or work, and simply ask what's possible.

Example Prompt:

"I've never really used AI before. I'm a [your role] with about [X] years of experience, and I'm curious how tools like ChatGPT could actually help someone like me.
Ask me a few questions to learn more about my situation, and then suggest practical ways I could start using AI in my daily work or personal life."

That one prompt can open an entire learning path since you're asking the AI to help *you figure out what to ask next.*

Closing Reflection

"AI won't replace your judgment, but it can expand your perspective."

Start simple. Stay curious. Refine your questions as you go.

That's how *The Adaptive Professional* begins every new conversation, with **context, clarity, and purpose.**

Appendix C: Productive Prompts for Reinvention

(A Practical Starting Guide for The Adaptive Professional)

How to Use AI Effectively

If you've made it this far, you already know that adaptability isn't just about learning new tools, it's about learning how to think with them. For many mid-career professionals, AI can feel intimidating at first. But tools like ChatGPT aren't just for programmers or tech experts, they're conversation partners that can help you clarify ideas, plan next steps, and accelerate your growth.

Here's the secret: **AI only works as well as the context you give it.**

If you tell it nothing, it will guess. But if you tell it who you are, what you're working on, and what you want, it will adapt to you. Think of it as a digital colleague who's brilliant but knows absolutely nothing about you until you speak up.

A good first message to AI usually includes:

Your role or background ("I've been a project manager for 12 years in construction…").

Your current challenge or goal ("I'm considering a career pivot and want help exploring options.").

The type of help you want ("Please suggest ideas and a short action plan.").

You don't need perfect grammar or formatting. You just need honesty and enough context for the AI to work with.

Over time, you'll learn how to refine your questions to get sharper, more personal answers, a skill that will only grow in value as AI continues to evolve.

Below are ten high-value prompt areas, the kinds of professional crossroads nearly everyone encounters at some point. Each includes starter templates you can use directly or modify. Treat them as conversation openers, not one-time questions. After the AI responds, keep going. Ask "Can you expand on that?" or "Show me examples."
That's how you build momentum, one adaptive prompt at a time.

---

1. Career Reinvention & Identity Shift

When you're considering change, clarity begins with self-understanding.
Try this:

"I'm a mid-career professional with about [X] years of experience in [your field]. My current resume is attached [upload here]. I'm exploring new directions but unsure what fits my experience, skills and interests. Can you help me identify three alternative career paths I might consider, and describe what experiences and skills would transfer well into each?"

"As a follow up, please revise my resume to adapt to a potential job announcement for a [new role] in [new field]. Ask me any questions to best position my experience in a new industry and role."

"Here's a quick list of my strengths, interests, and what I want less of in my next job: [list them]. Help me write a one-paragraph career vision that feels authentic and exciting."

---

2. Learning New Technologies (Especially AI)

If you're feeling behind on new tools, you're not, you just need a map.
Try this:

"I'm in [your industry or job title], and I want to stay relevant as AI and automation expand. Based on what you know, what are five tools or skills I should focus on learning first, and what free resources could help me start?"

"I'd like to create a 30-day plan to become more confident using AI tools at work. Here's my current comfort level: [describe]. Please outline a step-by-step beginner roadmap."

---

3. Job Loss or Career Stagnation

When momentum stalls, it's time to rebuild purpose and confidence.
Try this:

"I recently left a job (or feel stuck in my current one). Here's my background: [describe]. Help me write a short, positive narrative that explains my transition and highlights my strengths for future interviews."

"I want to create a daily 10-minute routine for rebuilding professional momentum. Here's what my mornings look like. Can you design something realistic that helps me move forward?"

---

4. Financial Pressure & Midlife Money Reassessment

AI can help you see your full picture and plan better, even with limited details.
Try this:

"Here's my approximate financial picture: [income range, debts, savings, goals]. Help me identify three key areas I should focus on over the next year to create more stability and flexibility."

"Create a simple monthly financial checkup routine I can follow, something that keeps me aware without feeling overwhelmed."

---

5. Burnout, Stress, and Redefining Success

Sometimes it's not the work that's broken, it's how we're doing it.
Try this:

"I'm feeling burned out and unmotivated in my current role. Here's a brief description of what's draining me. Can you help me reframe my week to restore some balance and meaning?"

"Help me define what 'success' should look like in this next phase of my life. Here's what currently matters most to me: [list priorities]."

---

6. Leadership Fatigue & Transition

Great leadership now means adaptability, empathy, and clarity, not control.
Try this:

"I lead a team of [X] people in [industry]. Lately I've felt disconnected and less effective. Based on that, what leadership adjustments or habits could help me re-engage my team?"

"Help me design a 15-minute team meeting format that feels energizing and future-focused rather than routine."

---

7. Purpose & Impact

Meaningful work often starts with rediscovering your "why."
Try this:

"Here's what I do for a living: [describe]. I want to connect it more deeply to something meaningful. Based on this, can you help me articulate a short personal mission statement?"

"Suggest three ways someone with my skills could make a positive impact in my community or profession without leaving my current role."

---

8. Entrepreneurship & Independent Work

AI is an incredible brainstorming partner for testing and validating ideas.
Try this:

"I'm considering starting a side business or consulting service. Here's my background: [brief summary]. What are five business ideas that align with my experience and market trends?"

"Help me outline a 90-day experiment to test one business idea without risking my full-time income."

---

9. Balancing Family, Aging Parents & Career Goals

Balance doesn't mean doing everything, it means knowing what matters most right now.
Try this:

"Here's what my weekly responsibilities look like: family, work, and personal time. Can you suggest small schedule adjustments that could create more balance or breathing room?"

"Help me design a realistic personal boundary plan that protects time for family and health without hurting my career."

---

10. Reclaiming Confidence & Reinvention Narrative

The story you tell about yourself shapes what's possible next.
Try this:

"Here's my professional journey in a few sentences: [describe]. I want to reframe it as a growth story, one that shows resilience and adaptability. Can you help me rewrite it that way?"

"Help me list three short phrases or affirmations I can use to remind myself of my strengths when I'm doubting my direction."

Closing Note

AI isn't magic, it's leverage. It helps you think faster, see clearer, and act sooner. The more honestly you describe your situation, the better it can support your next move.

You don't need to sound like an expert, just start the conversation.

Your adaptability begins the moment you do.

Appendix D: Adaptive Action Plan

Your Personal Roadmap for Growing with AI

The Adaptive Action Plan (AAP) is a simple, practical tool designed to help anyone begin using AI with confidence, no matter your starting point. You don't need to be technical, and you don't need to understand every tool. This plan breaks AI adoption into small, manageable steps so you can learn at your own pace, experiment safely, and build real skills over time. Use it to explore new tools, improve everyday tasks, spark creativity, or reduce the work that drains your time. The AAP works for professionals, students, job seekers, and anyone curious about using AI to work smarter. Fill out this template honestly, revisit it often, and treat it as a living document. As you grow, your plan grows with you.

---

1. Your Vision & Values

What do you want to achieve? Why does it matter to you? (Example: "Be more efficient at work," "Have more confidence using new tools," "Spend less time on repetitive tasks.")

My vision:

My values (what guides me):

---

2. Task & Skill Inventory

List your regular tasks and identify which could benefit from AI. (Example: drafting emails, reports, lesson plans, customer feedback analysis.)

Current tasks:

____

____

Tasks AI could help with:

____

____

Skills or tools I need to explore:

____

____

____

3. My First Small Experiment

Choose ONE task to test with AI this week. (Keep it small, simple, and low-pressure.)

My experiment:

____

____

AI tool(s) I'll use:

____

Deadline: ______________________

____

4. Feedback & Reflection

After completing your experiment, note what worked and what didn't.

What went well:

____

____

Challenges or surprises:

____

____

What I learned:

____

____

____

5. Adjust & Try Again

How will you improve the next attempt?

My next step:

____

____

Adjustment(s) I'll make:

____

____

____

6. Collaborate & Share

Who can I talk with? Who can help me stay motivated? (Colleagues, friends, online groups, class partners.)

People or communities I'll share with:

____

____

____

7. Human-Centered Check

Does this use of AI serve people well? Is it ethical, empathetic, and aligned with my values?

My human-centered check:

____

____

____

My AAP Summary (One Sentence)

Complete this after finishing the page.

"Over the next 30 days, I will use AI to

____,

because

____."

About the Author

David G. Gatchell is a proud father of two wonderful children, financial literacy, tech fluency, and entrepreneurship educator, author, and creator of tools that help people break free from economic struggle. He is the author of *The Financial Empowerment Handbook*, the foundational text for his financial literacy programs taught to schools and diverse community groups across the country, and the financial literacy parable, *Steps to Prosperity*.

David is the founder of Four Gifts Publishing, a platform dedicated to developing relatable, high-impact financial education materials. He also created the Finance IQ Test, a first-of-its-kind diagnostic tool that measures financial knowledge and decision-making in real-world scenarios.

As the Founder and Executive Director of nonprofit Prospera Literacy, David leads community-focused initiatives that promote both financial and technical fluency, two pillars he believes are essential to prosperity in the modern world.

Motivated by his own early struggles and driven by a deep desire to level the playing field, David's mission is simple: make prosperity possible for everyone, especially those who've been left out of the conversation for far too long.

A Note from the Publisher

Thank you for reading *The Adaptive Professional.* We hope Alex's story offered more than inspiration, that it gave you perspective, encouragement, and a renewed confidence in your ability to adapt and thrive in an age of rapid change.

At Four Gifts Publishing, our mission is to help people build lives of confidence, adaptability, and lasting freedom, financially, professionally, and personally. We believe knowledge should empower action, and that stories can help bridge the gap between understanding and doing.

If you'd like to continue exploring the themes of personal growth and practical life skills, we invite you to discover our other titles:

The Financial Empowerment Handbook: a straightforward guide to mastering personal finance, saving, spending, and building long-term stability.

Steps to Prosperity: a modern parable about breaking harmful financial habits, developing a healthier money mindset, and building a better life.

Together, these books, like *The Adaptive Professional*, are written to help readers make sense of a changing world and move forward with clarity, confidence, and purpose.

The Team at Four Gifts Publishing
Empowering people to learn, adapt, and thrive.

www.ingramcontent.com/pod-product-compliance
Lightning Source LLC
LaVergne TN
LVHW100308210926
848480LV00003B/1064

* 9 7 9 8 9 8 6 7 2 0 0 4 3 *